Derry
Down the Days

Philip Cunningham

First published in November 2002 by
Guildhall Press, Unit 4, Ráth Mór Centre,
Bligh's Lane, Derry BT48 0LZ
T: (028) 7136 4413 F: (028) 7137 2949
info@ghpress.com www.ghpress.com

ISBN 0 946451 70 2

Printed in Republic of Ireland by ColourBooks Limited, Dublin

Acknowledgements

Thanks to May and Frank Curran and Garbhan Downey, editor of the *Derry News*, for taking an interest in my written memories of childhood, and for publishing the articles weekly in the newspaper.

I am extremely grateful to The Ulster Local History Trust, Downpatrick, and to Derry City Council Heritage and Museum Service, for their generous grants towards publication.

My appreciations are also due to: Maura Craig, Dick Sinclair and the staff of the Central Library, Foyle Street, for their kind help in allowing me to browse at will through their photographic archives; Lewis Childs, Librarian at Magee College, for his permission to view the Magee Community Collection; Eamon and Dr Martin Melaugh for images from the CAIN website; David Bigger, *Derry News* and Willie Carson family for images from their collections.

For professional help and advice, thanks to Paul Hippsley and Joe McAllister of Guildhall Press.

Thanks to all the people who permitted me to use their precious photographs: Aidan Gallagher, Patricia Coyle, Jimmy Doherty, Phil Donaghy, Gerry Downey, John McGinley, Charley Logue, Canon the Rev Fr Canning, Doreen Rice Wray, Patricia McAdams, Patricia Ward, Mickey McGinley, Margaret Brown, Mrs Stanley, Leo Coyle, Mickey Gillespie, John McCloskey, Eddie Moore, Eamon McDowell, Bobby Coyle, Willie Breslin, Bernadette Morrison and Nan Hill.

Finally, I have to thank my patient wife Rosita for spending so much time reading the original unedited scribbling for my manuscript.

This publication was produced with financial assistance from:

The Ulster Local
History Trust

Derry City Council's Heritage
and Museum Service

*for my family,
old back of the
walls neighbours
and friends.*

Foreword

Why should anyone be interested in what took place on a couple of little city side streets more than half a century ago? That was the question that shot through my head when veteran journalist Frank Curran introduced me to Philip Cunningham in the summer of 2001. Phil, I was told, had written an account of his childhood in the long-since disappeared Friel's Terrace and Nailor's Row area. We might want to publish it in the *Derry News*... Hold the front page, I thought.

Then, however, when the pair had left the office, I glanced at the manuscript – and before I'd finished the first page, I was a convert. I think it was his humour that grabbed me first – the razor-sharp insights into the mischievous world of the urchin child. I loved the style too; gentle, innocent narrative – homely and homespun. Another charm was the recognition of a common Derry history. I met characters my father and grandfather might have known personally – and even if they didn't, they knew people like them.

Some of the vignettes were familiar too – anecdotes almost myth-like in their universal appeal. For a while, I thought Phil might have remained the *Derry News's* best-kept secret, his 'Derry Down the Days' column (effectively this book in serial form) the preserve of the older, less cynical reader.

I couldn't have been more wrong. Time without number, hard-nosed news lovers when talking about the paper would inform me: "And do you know what I love most about the *Derry News...*" before singing the joys of the Cunningham reminisces. Most of all, however, Phil's column and this book, gave me a chance to get to know him. And his visits to the office for tea, chat and craic became the high point of my working week.

It is rare in this world that you get a chance to make a new friend you're sure you've known all your life. Read this book and you've found one.

Garbhan Downey
Editor, *Derry News*

Contents

Introduction

I suppose it is a natural human trait for people to begin reminiscing when they get older and for their children to get fed up listening to the same old stories about "the good old days". I remember in my youth listening to my own parents and grandparents relating events from their past and thinking to myself, "here we go again." However, after they were no longer with us, I regretted that I had never recorded some of their life experiences.

This is what prompted me to begin writing some of my own memories of my life from 1937 until I was twelve years old when I lived with my family in Friel's Terrace in Nailor's Row, facing Derry's Walls and overlooking the Bogside. I wanted to capture these memories for my children and give them a flavour of the events, people and conditions I encountered in and around the city during those formative years.

"Has nobody in this street got a sweeping brush?" Friel's Terrace in the late 1920s. (Courtesy David Bigger collection.)

11

I had no intentions of having anything published until, fortunately, I casually mentioned my scribbling to May Curran who introduced me to her husband Frank, a renowned journalist in the city for over 60 years. I was slightly embarrassed but delighted to learn that Frank had enjoyed my work and had passed it over to the editor of the *Derry News*, Garbhan Downey, who serialised it in his weekly newspaper.

As my articles emerged, more and more memories came back to me and friends and neighbours would remind me of even more characters or events I had forgotten. As a result, the articles developed into a collection of memories that were not necessarily linked from week to week. Garbhan then introduced me to Guildhall Press with a view to publishing and their professional touch has sewn my patchwork of stories and pictures together to produce this treasured book.

I hope this explains, to some degree at least, the somewhat random order of the book's contents. At the same time, I hope it does not detract from your enjoyment of the memories I would like to share about an earlier generation's simpler but harder times in the city.

The characters and neighbours I mention in this memoir, some of whom I do not name as a matter of courtesy, form a major part of my childhood memories. I have a great deal of fondness and respect for each one of them and I am proud and privileged to have known and lived among them.

My House, Home and Family

Friel's Terrace was a row of nine houses in the middle of Nailor's Row, known locally as 'The Back of the Walls' because it ran parallel to, and facing, the exterior western side of Derry's Walls from Butcher's Gate to Long Tower Street at the Double Bastion. Just past the lower end of Friel's Terrace, and facing Paddy 'Peggy' Strain's house at number twenty-three, was the Royal Bastion with Governor George Walker's Pillar. The bastion pushed out the lower middle of Nailor's Row, causing the road to veer right at the top of Primrose Lane, an old cobbled track that curved down the banking. The lane emerged between two houses – McVicker's at the bottom of Fahan Street and a tenement house at the beginning of St Columb's Wells. The banking is the steep grassy slope that runs down from the Walls to St Columb's Wells, just on the edge of the Bogside, which derived its name from a marshy stretch of land once known as the cow bog.

The Cunningham household in their back yard in Friel's Terrace in 1945. Back row, from left to right: father, Susie, baby Hughie, mother. Middle: Freddie, Danny and author. Front: Mary, Margaret and Helen.

13

Number two Friel's Terrace was my home from my birth in 1937. It was a two-storey house with two bedrooms upstairs and a front sitting room-cum-bedroom and a back living room downstairs where the cooking, washing and all the general household chores were done daily. There was no sink or indoor running water, the toilet and water tap being in the back yard. In winter, the tap would sometimes freeze up and my father would have to thaw it out using a burning, rolled-up newspaper.

At one time, there were eighteen people living in the house: my father and mother; three brothers, four sisters and myself; three half-brothers and one half-sister; and an uncle and an aunt on my mother's side who were both unmarried. Two cousins also lived with us and all were loved and cared for as one big family.

My mother's maiden name was Cassie Cooley and my father Paddy, who worked for the Derry Gaslight Company, was a gas fitter/plumber. I went to the Convent of Mercy School on Artillery Street with my brothers Freddie and Danny, sisters Susie, Margaret, Mary and Helen, and cousin Bridget Lynch. After two years, I was transferred to the Brow of the Hill Christian Brothers' School (CBS) at the bottom of Hogg's Folly. My youngest brother Hughie was a Down's syndrome baby who died suddenly when he was three years old – one little soul gone, leaving seventeen of us in number two Friel's Terrace. Another half-sister, Rosie, lived in Sloan's Terrace with her aunt, Pearl Carlin.

My Uncle Freddie Cooley worked in Doherty's scrap yard on Foyle Street and my Aunt Julia Cooley, his sister, worked for a long time in the Strand Cinema restaurant. As for my half-brothers: Paddy drove a fruit lorry for Bannigan's of Foyle Street; Willie worked as an apprentice plumber along with my father; and Mickey was training to be a male nurse in the mental asylum on Strand Road until he went into St Columb's chest hospital with TB (tuberculosis). My half-sister Kathleen worked in one of the many shirt factories that employed thousands of women from the city and neighbouring towns and villages around Derry. Two cousins, Willie Cooley and Bridget Lynch, whose mothers died soon after their births, also lived with us. Willie was a barber in Willman's hairdressers in Waterloo Square.

There were many more houses in the area that contained three or four different families living under the one roof. Next door to us, in

Author's father Paddy and mother Cassie dolled up on their wedding day in 1934.

number one, were Carlin, Logue and Doherty; in number seven were Feeney and Lynch. Then there were Doherty and McGinley in number eight, next door to the McCay, McFarland and Watt families.

Our house, like everybody else's, had no electricity, and when it grew dark my father or my Uncle Freddie would light the gaslight. Every house had gas piped to it for lighting and cooking. Most people cooked and boiled water over the open fire, and some of them also had a gas ring that connected with a flexible tube to the mains. We were lucky with my father working for the Gaslight Company, because he was able to get a second-hand gas cooker and install it himself.

Most of the houses in Friel's Terrace had an iron range with the fire section open at the top, and across the throat of the chimney was an iron bar from which you could hang pots for cooking or the kettle to boil over the fire. There was an oven at the side of the fire where women would bake scones and cakes and buns. We used to put nine or ten spuds into it during the day. Then at night, we would sit in front of the fire when all the adults were out at the pictures, or at evening devotions in the Long Tower Church, and eat them with a nice drink of buttermilk. They tasted scrumptious!

I remember the day when my brother Freddie and I hung a cloth doll belonging to our sister Susie on the iron bar over the fire. As we watched it burn, we didn't realise how bad we must have been, not until Susie walked in and saw her favourite doll blazing fiercely up the chimney and nearly broke her heart crying. There were no spuds and buttermilk for Freddie and me that night when we were put to bed earlier than usual.

Derry's Walls and Walker Unarmed

Just twenty feet from our front door loomed the grey-green stonework of Derry's Walls. To our left, the Royal Bastion jutted out with its cannons pointing through the embrasures. One aimed up the street towards the Double Bastion at the top of Nailor's Row where another cannon, Roaring Meg, poked its long, black shining barrel from the ramparts westward over the rooftops towards the Lone Moor Road and

Walker's Pillar, the Apprentice Boys' Memorial Hall and the spire of St Columb's Church of Ireland Cathedral dominate the skyline above Friel's Terrace and Nailor's Row. Johnny McDermott's shed is on the right (1940s). (Watercolour by author.)

Governor George Walker's statue atop the 100-ft column in Royal Bastion on
Derry's Walls, overlooking Nailor's Row and the Bogside in the late 1940s. Standing
at their door are Josie Dean and his wife. (Courtesy David Bigger collection.)

18

to the horizon, where King James and his army camped during the Great Siege of Derry in 1689.

Walker's Pillar towered more than 100 feet above on the Royal Bastion. Atop stood our silent unmoving neighbour, Governor Reverend George Walker, hero of the Great Siege, with his back to me and his left arm extended, pointing towards Boom Hall down on the banks of the River Foyle. In his right hand he grasped a bible. At his back rose a flagpole with the Union flag of Britain fluttering from it eastwards towards the Apprentice Boys' Memorial Hall with its own Derry Crimson flag flying above the roof.

Governor Walker's statue originally had a sword in its left hand, but both fell off during a storm in the late 1800s – contrary to local legend that claims they were knocked off by a particularly accurate stone thrower from Nelson Street. The sword is now in the Chapter Room of St Columb's Cathedral. A spiral of 110 stone steps inside the pillar allowed any energetic climber to reach the railed platform at the top where Walker's statue stood.

Games, Relatives and Streets

My Aunt Jane, she called me in, she gave me tea in her wee tin.
Half a bap with sugar on the top and three wee sweetie balls after that.
She told me to go home and I wouldn't go, so she shut the door on my big toe.
Ho, ho, ho, that's too sore, I'm not going back to my aunt's anymore.

Frequently we used the cannon mouths on the Walls as targets for a game in which we would try to throw stones into them; the best of five throws was the winner. We also threw stones at Walker's statue; innocent fun then, as we had no malicious intent, but today it would be regarded as vandalism. Anyone who could climb to the gun ports or portholes at the top of the Walls was considered a good climber and very brave. We didn't overdo the praise, for we knew that one day we would all be able to perform the same feat.

We bought our spinning tops in Johnny Larmour's shop down near Butcher's Gate. The spinning top was shaped like a mushroom with a metal stud on the bottom and it had to be struck with a whip in order to make it spin. To spin them, we went down to the Lecky Road because it had a flat tarred surface.

Another game we played was to curl up inside a big lorry tyre and roll down the steep slope of the banking. Most times, we would fall out of the tyre as it bounced down towards the back yards of St Columb's Wells and two tries were enough to leave one with skinned knees and elbows.

My sisters played hopscotch on the footpath, chalking out numbered squares and using a shoe-polish tin as a marker. They also played rope skipping with their friends and sang various skipping rhymes such as "On the mountain stands a lady; who she is I do not know", as each one of the girls jumped over the rope in turn.

From our back windows, I overlooked our playground, the grassy banking where we played Cowboys and Indians, hunters throwing spears, and Japs and Americans with bombs made of grass sods. We would also slide down the steep slopes of the banking sitting on dockers' shovels in summer and sleighs made from sheets of tin all the year round.

From these same upstairs back windows we also looked directly down over the streets that are now the Bogside: Nelson Street, Wellington Street, Blucher Street, St Columb's Wells, Fahan Street, Lecky Road, and Fox's Corner. All my relatives lived in those small streets below. In Fox's Corner lived my cousins, the Lynches, and Aunt Susan, my mother's sister. Susan died when her baby Bridget was just a few months old; my mother then reared Bridget with us. Jimmy, Bridget's half-brother, was my close pal and childhood companion until we reached manhood. My Granda and Granny Cunningham lived on the Lecky Road, and my uncles and aunts lived in many of the surrounding streets. Cousin Kitty McKane lived in the house at the corner of St Columb's Street and Lecky Road, the gable end of which is known throughout the world today as Free Derry Corner. My cousins, the McCaffertys and McGinleys, lived a couple of streets above in Blucher Street.

To the left were: Howard Street (where my Uncle John Cunningham lived), Lone Moor Road (where my Uncle Hugh Cooley lived),

A packed Harp's Hall in Deanery Place in the 1950s with my sister Susie, Kay Cooley, Betty Dillon, Winnie and Danny Cooley, 'Stoll' Doherty and Kathleen Kivelehan (née McCarron) in the front row. Middle right is 'Governor' Doherty's mum and Paddy 'Ducksy' Cassidy. (Courtesy Willie Carson collection.)

Reflection of Saint Eugene's Cathedral in the Bull Reservoir, owned by Andrew Watt's Distillery, on the Lone Moor Road.

Stanley's Walk, Elmwood Street, Beechwood Street, Limewood Street, and beyond that, the Brandywell (where my Uncle Eddie Cooley lived). We loved to visit his little house in Deanery Street where we were always warmly welcomed by our cousins, Danny, Jack, Tommy, Tess, Winnie and Kathleen, whose mother had died at an early age. My other cousins, the Downeys and McCools, also lived in the Brandywell.

In the hazy distance lay Foyle Hill, the 'Green Hill Far Away' that inspired Mrs Cecil Frances Alexander to write the famous hymn of the same name (and the equally famous *All Things Bright and Beautiful*) in the nineteenth century. She died in 1895 and her grave is marked with a white cross in the old ground in the City Cemetery.

To our right could be seen Watt's Distillery and William Street, with a maze of little streets around it running into the distance towards the Northland Road and away towards the River Foyle and Pennyburn.

Dominating the surroundings was the majestic spire of St Eugene's Cathedral, and above it on the horizon, a line of tall trees where Creggan Estate is today. Little did I know then that one day (when I was twelve) I would be living there in number forty-four Dunree Gardens.

Close by was Walker's Square and, rising above the rooftops, the green dome of our parish church of St Columba, which we called the Long Tower.

Larmour's 'Comfooterments' and an Eerie Midnight Visitor

In numbers one and two at the bottom of Nailor's Row, near Butcher's Gate, was Johnny Larmour's house shop. He sold everything from a needle to an anchor and hung his wares on Derry's Walls. Pots, pans, chairs, tables, ropes, three-legged iron pots, cartwheels, horse harnesses, Moses baskets and a whole lot of other 'comfooterments'. I remember looking in his window at wooden spinning tops, glass marbles, a dartboard, chessmen, tin boxes and various other oddments of all colours, shapes and sizes. They were only small houses, but his was known far and wide as 'Larmour's, where one could get a bargain.'

'Comfooterments' lie against the Walls outside Johnny Larmour's house on lower Nailor's Row, near Butcher's Gate (1940s).

Paddy Dean, a neighbour of Larmour's, lived in an even smaller single-storey house and was reputed to be the tallest man in Derry at seven feet. Every Mayday, Paddy hung a branch of a whinbush outside his front door, and sometimes even his neighbours' doors. It was an old Irish tradition to ward off evil spirits from animals and inhabitants. At the end of the day, all the whins were taken down and burned at the bottom of the street.

Paddy Dean used to play cards with his friends at home in the winter evenings. On one such occasion, an unsettling event is rumoured to have taken place as the men were all seated around the table playing poker in the living room. The stakes were never high because money was scarce, and the men really only gathered to chat and pass the time. As they played and chatted on this particular evening, the clock on the mantelpiece chimed the hour of midnight, considered a very eerie time in those days because people were very superstitious. As the last chime faded, a stranger wearing a top hat and a black cloak about his shoulders entered the room and asked to be included in the game. The men obliged, making room for the new arrival and dealing him a hand of cards. As they played and chatted amongst themselves, the stranger just sat there listening without uttering a word.

When the first game ended with the 'quiet man' winning, the dealer, who was seated next to him, was gathering up the playing cards when one dropped onto the floor at his feet. When he bent down to pick it up, he let out a terrible scream and the stranger suddenly stood up and rushed out of the house. After the commotion died down and the dealer had recovered, he told the onlookers that when he had bent down to pick up the fallen card (which was the ace of spades), he was shocked to see that the stranger did not have normal human feet, but instead had two cloven hooves. It was also said that two women coming across the street at the time saw a ball of fire burst out of the door and career down the banking towards Fox's Corner. That episode finished the playing of cards in Paddy Dean's house for good.

Other Nailor's Row Neighbours

Tommy Doughan lived in number twenty and he never came out of the house in daylight. He had a long white beard, and we often saw him during the day looking out of his back-bedroom window. He made us feel so afraid that we could barely look up at him as we played on the banking. After midnight, he could be seen walking along the top of the banking, or down along Derry's Walls.

Another person who frequented the top of the Walls was 'Wee' Johnny Nicholl from Nelson Street. Because of his short stature, he

Plenty to talk about at the top of Howard's Street in the 1950s. Included are Neilly Diven, W 'Budgim' Callaghan and Johnny McFadden. The two women conversing are Myra Connor and Nora Diven. (Courtesy Patricia Deery.)

George and Jimmy Doherty guarding their wee cousins, the Quigley brothers, in the back yard of number one Friel's Terrace in the late 1950s. (Courtesy Jimmy Doherty.)

couldn't see over the Walls and used to stand looking through the gun ports. Wee Johnny always kept his hands up inside his sleeves and held his arms behind his back. We believed that he was hiding a knife there, so we ran away whenever we saw him. If a young child was disobedient or naughty, its parents would say, "I'll get Johnny Nicholl to you," so the child would behave itself.

In reality, Johnny was just another harmless unemployed man passing the time and walking around the Derry Walls as part of his daily routine.

At the top of Nailor's Row, in two houses just before turning right into Walker's Square, was Annie Barr's lodging house. It accommodated over thirty lodgers, mostly impoverished men, who were continuously coming and going. Annie regularly made soup for her lodgers, and she would pass around whatever was left over to her neighbours who were very glad to get it. Andy Hegarty, a close neighbour, remembered that a bed for a night in Annie's cost tuppence and added that she was a very kind and generous woman.

In the late evenings, men would gather at the gable end of Annie's house to chat about sport and news and have a bit of craic. Very few people owned a radio (television had yet to be invented), so people made their own entertainment such as singing, either individually or in small groups in harmony. It was lovely and peaceful lying in bed listening to them singing outside. Similar scenes occurred all around Derry at that time.

Modest People and Mayors

There were a few families who lived in Nailor's Row who went quietly about their daily business and whose children were much older than we were, so we didn't have much contact with them. The Carlins at the bottom of the street had five sons and one daughter. Mickey, the youngest of them, was a year older than me and sold *Belfast Telegraph* newspapers along with two of his older brothers in the town centre. He, like his brothers, was a giant for his age and was too big to play games with us.

John 'The Narrowman' Martin lived in an upstairs bedroom next door to us in number three. He wore a brimmed hat, neat short jacket and trousers, and spats and leggings. His moustache was waxed at the ends and he carried a silver-handled walking stick that he clicked on the ground with every smart step he took. He was a very slim and tidy figure of a man who minded his own business and never spoke or glanced at us children as he came and went.

Rose Anne Harper made vestments for the priests of the parish and did a lot of charity work. Whenever anybody was dying and waiting for the priest to come to give them the Last Rites, Rose was sent for. She would lay the bedside table with a white cloth, then set it with the crucifix and the holy water and the lighted holy candles. When the person died, Rose washed and dressed the corpse and laid it out on the bed for the wake.

The Ramsey, Tierney, Kerr and Crumley families also lived in the general area and each of them had a family member become mayor of the city in later years.

Kites, Friends and the 'Bars'

There was a family near the top of Nailor's Row called Commander, and the father, a former English sailor and very friendly man, made coloured kites. They were so well made, with fine sticks and light paper, that people from all over Derry bought them and admired them – and they were great to fly. We could fly them high above the banking, even higher than Governor Walker, and far higher than any buildings down in the Bogside. But if the string broke, the kites would plummet into some street below, never to be seen again.

Other families who lived near the top of Nailor's Row that I remember with fondness, and who were very kind to us younger ones, were the Tierneys, Diamonds and McGlincheys.

Minnie McGlinchey, who frequented our house every day, was a very close companion and lifelong friend to my mother and Aunt Julia. We loved to listen to her as she sat by our fireside every evening telling us the local news and incidents of that day. That kind of information and conversation was called the 'bars', so whenever someone wished to relate an important piece of local news or scandal, they would begin by saying, "Wait till I tell you the bars."

Minnie's sister Kitty married an English serviceman, Andy Reid, who was killed in the Second World War. They had one son, called John, who became an excellent footballer. John was more commonly called Andy and was signed in 1955 by West Ham United, then managed by Ted Fenton.

Debt Collectors, Snuff and Pos

Dawson Noble from the Lone Moor Road came into our house every Friday to collect life assurance payments from my mother. He performed in all the local concerts and pantomimes and was a good baritone. Instead of him knocking at the door, he started to sing as he came into the house along the front hallway and kept on singing as he stood in the middle of the living-room floor. Everybody enjoyed his little weekly performance before he went on to tell the latest bars.

Newly ordained Father Bernard Canning from Nelson Street with some of his old neighbours and friends from the surrounding areas in the 1950s. Included are: D Doherty, Frankie Doherty, J McGlinchey, Gerry Hegarty, Ted O'Neil, Alex O'Neill, Denis Harkin, Ted McGinley, John 'Danno' Feeney, John McGinley, W 'Farouk' Stewart, Joe Ferry, Neil McCann, Jim McBride, 'Jimbo' Harkin, Johnny McFadden, J Hegarty, F McCloskey and Bill McDaid. (Courtesy John McGinley.)

30

A small man who lived in Henrietta Street called Bobby O'Donnell also collected money every Friday evening for Hill's clothes shop. Whenever Bobby got his money, he took a little silver box from his waistcoat pocket, opened the lid and went round the room offering everyone a pinch of snuff. Then he took a large pinch between his forefinger and thumb and sniffed it up each of his nostrils. By the time he left, everybody in the house was sneezing.

As all the houses had their toilet in the back yard, it was awkward when you had to go in the middle of the night. Every household, therefore, owned a po (a chamber pot), some fancily designed, but most of them just plain white. These fitted neatly under the beds and were only used to pee in. In the morning, the po was discreetly taken downstairs when no strangers were about and the contents poured down the toilet. Many houses just used a galvanised tin bucket at night that was placed on the landing for everybody's use; not very pleasant, but the reality of the times.

Eerie Experiences

Every Catholic home in Derry (and probably Ireland!) had a print of Jesus of the Sacred Heart hanging above the mantelpiece. It portrayed Jesus with small flames surrounding his heart, holding out his hands to reveal the bleeding wounds from the nails that crucified him. It was scary whenever you were in the room alone because no matter where you moved to, his eyes followed you (or so it seemed!). It was more eerie at dusk with the ticking of the clock on the mantelshelf making the little hairs stand on the back of my neck before I scampered out to the front door to the safety of my mother and the rest of the family.

There was a very poor family who lived in Nailor's Row and some of my pals and I played with their children who were around our own ages. Some nights we went into their front downstairs room where we all had to sit on the floor because there were no chairs. They had no lights in the room so a big fire would be burning in the grate. The flames danced up the chimney, and we would sit in front of it on the floor watching our shadows flickering across the ceiling, listening to

Saint Mary's Accordion Band, playing for the residents of Nelson Street and Blucher Street in June 1956 with bandsman Willie Healey in the centre. Also included: Maureen McGinley, Johnny Healey, Ted O'Neil, J McCay in doorway, John Doherty, B McGlinchey, Frankie Doherty, 'Jimbo' Harkin and John 'Danno' Feeney. (Courtesy Rev B Canning.)

ghost stories, with the shivers running up our spines and the hairs standing on our heads. Then, when it was time to go home, we would run up through the eerie darkness below the Walls, praying that a ghost wouldn't jump out and grab us.

Paddy Strain and Walker's Square

"Shipquay Street's a slippy street to slide upon."
A popular local tongue twister.

One evening Paddy Strain, a big, strong, blond-haired man, was standing with some friends outside Annie Barr's house at the top of the street. Paddy casually pulled the *Belfast Telegraph* from his coat pocket and began reading aloud from it to his companions. They all listened intently to the stories about a horse that had slipped on Shipquay Street and bolted into the River Foyle, and about a boat sinking down at the quay with twenty dockers onboard, and some other funny incidents that everyone assumed were in the newspaper. Everybody was having a good laugh until one man said to him, "Paddy, that newspaper you're

On the left is a part of upper Nailor's Row and, from the top of the banking looking towards Walker's Square, the dome of the Long Tower Church is in the distance. The Bonnar family lived at the left far end of the Square and the Young family in the first house on the right. Opposite Bonnar's was the flight of steps that went down to Howard's Place and Maggie 'Chuck' Campbell's front room sweetie shop (1940s). (Watercolour by author.)

Big Paddy 'Peggy' Strain in his pension years,
spinning a yarn to 'Doc' Doherty in the 1960s.

The Lecky Road in the 1960s.

reading is upside down." Everyone went silent and Paddy replied, "Sure any dog's arse can read it the right way up." Everyone laughed in agreement and urged him to 'read' on.

Annie Barr's son-in-law, Dan McGilloway, who lived on the middle of the brae leading down to Walker's Square, had a chip shop inside the shed between his house and his neighbours, the McCruddens. He only opened an odd night and on Friday and Saturday evenings. Everybody loved to get a bag of Dan's chips covered in salt and vinegar. The Hegarty family lived up the brae from Dan's, and Bosco, Charley and Andy were good amateur boxers at the time, as was Ming Harkin, who lived near them. They all trained in the cellars under the houses in Walker's Square. Andy went on to become North West Billiards Junior Champion in 1953 when he was only sixteen.

At the top of the brae, we would get a plate of beans or peas in Bella 'Butts' Doherty's front-room shop for a penny. It was a nice treat to stand at Bella's linoleum-covered counter, eating a plate of her delicious beans or peas, or a nice warm plate of soup on a cold day.

Willie Divine owned a public house on the brae at Walker's Square and in later years sold it to Bob Weir, an ex-merchant seaman who named the bar 'The Steamship Inn'. Bob was a long lanky man who wore a cap and always had a grey stubble beard. He never seemed to look clean or tidy and lived with Lily, his wife or partner, above the bar that was always very dirty. He was known to be a very charitable person who never refused to give alms to beggars or a free drink to a desperate, penniless alcoholic. There were no tumblers in the bar, and the clientele drank their beers and stout from the bottles; the cheap wines and whiskeys were mostly served in cups because there were only a few small glasses.

A few humorous exaggerated yarns about The Steamship Inn were being told at the time. One was about the day a passing stranger went into the bar and ordered a bottle of stout and demanded to have it poured into a glass, so Bob went out to the back room and brought him in a red glass which had a cross and the initials IHS (the first three letters in Greek of the name Jesus, often used as a Christian emblem) etched on it. The glass happened to be the colsa (cozzy) oil lamp that was supposed to be lit and placed in front of the Sacred Heart picture and the customer was satisfied with that.

Four handsome glamour boys outside McGinley's house in Nailor's Row in 1956. From left: Junior Good, James 'Brother' McGinley, Willie Breslin and Brian McGinley. (Courtesy Willie Breslin.)

Some residents of Nelson Street in the 1940s. From left: Sarah Gallagher, Cassie Anne McNutt, Sadie McCauley, Kathleen Johnston, Mary Anne Tyre, Teanie McDonagh, Mickey Duddy, Nellie O'Donnell, Cass O'Donnell, Margaret White and Bridgie Walsh. At the front: Pat Bradley, John Diven, William Thomas McLaughlin and Patrick O'Donnell. (Courtesy Rev B Canning.)

Bob's hands always looked black and dirty, and one day an American tourist went into the bar with one of the local men. When he came out of the bar after drinking a bottle of beer, he said to his friend that it was the first time that he had been served by an Irish barman who was wearing black gloves. We children loved listening to those old yarns and innocently believed them to be true.

One afternoon, as a friend and I walked over Foyle Street past the butter market, we saw a crowd of children following Bob as he went down Guildhall Street and on to the quayside. We followed them and heard Bob saying that he was going to jump into the River Foyle. When he reached the wharf, he stood at the edge for a few minutes, looking down into the river but didn't jump. Instead, he turned and walked back towards Foyle Street again with the children following him chanting, "Coward" and "Cowardy Custard" at him. We learned that he had had a row with Lily and was trying to frighten her to make her feel sorry for him.

At the bottom of the brae was Walker's Square with fifty houses. On one side stood about twenty older houses with cellars, backing on to the top of the banking. Professional people had owned these at one time. There were no walls between the cellars that had once been used to stable horses. I don't remember seeing any, but I often went into the cellars when they were used as a boxing gym to watch the bigger boys training. There was a single tap fixed to the outside front wall of one of the houses to provide water to that side of the street.

At the south end of the Square was a flight of steps that went down between two houses to Howard's Place, a cul-de-sac leading to Howard Street that ran down steeply to St Columb's Wells. In Howard's Place, Maggie Campbell's wee shop sold sweets that had to be smuggled into Derry because of the war rationing. Maggie got her supplies from Donegal just across the border in the 'Free State'. Maggie Campbell's was where we got our first-ever bubble gum and it was delicious.

At the northern end of the Square, on the banking side, was the ash pit where people dumped the ashes from their fires. In the winter, people would poke through these ashes and shake them through a griddle to find cinders to add to their fires along with whatever coal they could afford to buy.

There was a small stocky man who lived in the Square called Con Bonnar. He wore a brimmed hat and had leather leggings from his ankles to his knees. He had a big family and people were afraid of him because he had a reputation for fighting with anyone who crossed him. His wife was called Sally, and people said that they were very poor, as were many families in those days.

Another man in the Square, James Organ, made and sold wooden housey boards with numbers painted on them; housey was a game played like bingo.

Walker's Swifts was a very successful football team that won many trophies in the local competitions, and it fielded some fine and talented players who lived in the general area.

This is the first verse of a rhyme that some people sang about Walker's Square:

Oh, it's tough, mighty tough, in Walker's Square
But they always wash their face and comb their hair.
They all go to Mass on Sundays
And to Arthur's Pawn on Mondays.
Yes, it's tough, mighty tough, in Walker's Square.

The Black Pipe and Easter Hut Tragedies

A major feature of the banking was the huge black metal sewer pipe, about sixteen inches in diameter, that protruded from the top of the slope and ran about three or four feet above ground all the way to the bottom of the banking, a distance of fifty feet. Some days we played around that pipe for hours on end, sliding down it, climbing on it, falling off it and hiding behind it whenever the Indians or baddies were chasing us in one of our boyish games. It was known as the Black Pipe, and its metal top gleamed, polished by the many trousered backsides that had slid down it over the generations.

One day, a big white horse, belonging to Johnny McDermott from Nailor's Row, was grazing at the top of the banking beside the pipe, when it suddenly tumbled down the slope and broke its neck and died.

We all stood around watching in horror: it was sad to see the poor animal lying there with the blood trickling from its mouth and nose. Johnny had used the horse to pull his work cart that he kept in a shed on the top of the banking behind Friel's Terrace.

The Black Pipe was the cause of a tragic drowning in the 1960s when an employee of the Water Service was repairing an outlet pipe in a manhole at the bottom of the banking in St Columb's Wells. He was sitting in the manhole when a sudden rush of water came down the Black Pipe behind him and poured into it. His workmates and other people in the area tried to pull him out but were too late freeing his legs from the outlet pipe to save him. He was Wesley Bell from Bond Street in the Waterside, and I knew him personally from when I was sixteen and worked in the Atlantic Bar in Foyle Street.

It was near the same spot that a few boys from Walker's Square and Long Tower Street were digging a cave into the side of the slope to make an Easter hut, an old Irish tradition to represent Christ's empty tomb on the first Easter morning. When the cave was almost complete, one of the boys, Leo Young, noticed the roof beginning to sag. He warned his friend, Pat Cavanagh from Long Tower Street, about the danger, and Pat hurried out of the cave. Tragically, however, he went back in again to retrieve his mother's shovel that he had been using when suddenly the roof collapsed on top of him. The other boys couldn't rescue him, so they ran for help. When they eventually dug Pat out, he was dead. That was the last time anybody attempted to make an Easter hut or cave on the banking.

Tin Sheds

In St Columb's Wells at the bottom of the banking – between Denis Mc Monagle's in number thirty-two and Mrs Kane's in number thirty-four – was a tin shed where the Star billiards team practised for competitions. There was also another corrugated tin shed, between McShane's and Shields's houses, owned by Tony Begley, that was used as a bookie's; men passed the dark evenings in the shed chatting and playing cards. On a few occasions, we got up to mischief and threw stones down onto its tin

Jackie Kane from Nailor's Row on his hunkers (right) warms his hands at a fire on the banking in the 1950s. (Courtesy Patricia Deery.)

roof from the top of the banking to see who could hit it the most times. The stones bouncing off the sides and roof made a terrible racket and must have been ten times worse from inside the shed.

Sometimes, one or two of the braver men would emerge and dodge the hail of stones raining down from the top of the slope to chase us, and we would run off in fear in case they would catch and punish us. They never carried out the threat, however, and we realised in later years that the top of the banking was regarded as an unfriendly place for outsiders. At the same time, we didn't realise then that we were making a very dangerous nuisance of ourselves, and we really owed those inoffensive people an apology for annoying and endangering them with our thoughtless actions.

The Bells and Sunday Bests

Every evening at 9.00pm, a single bell could be heard tolling from somewhere deep behind Derry's Walls. It would ring for about ten minutes, a slow lonely melancholy sound, and we were told that it was the curfew bell. In the seventeenth century, the city fathers had imposed a curfew requiring Catholics to leave the walled city at nightfall and return to their homes in the countryside. Although the curfew itself had ended a long time ago, the traditional curfew bell was still sounded right up until the early 1960s.

On Sunday mornings, the bells of St Columb's Cathedral would chime; there must have been about ten of them, all pulled with ropes, and they had a nice, cheerful, melodious sound. The bells of St Eugene's Cathedral would play hymn tunes at Mass times, and at noon every day they chimed out that lovely hymn, *The Bells of the Angelus*. Sunday was a quiet restful day; no one did any work and none of the shops opened. People didn't sew or knit or do any kind of housework; even some of Sunday's dinner was cooked or prepared on Saturday night.

Everybody got washed, polished their shoes or brogues, and laid out their Sunday clothes on Saturday nights. The girls wore flouncy dresses and the boys wore ganseys (jumpers) and short trousers that were held up with gallasses (braces). The men's shirts were smoothed and the

Shortly after the ordination of Father Daniel 'Junior' Canning from Blucher Street, a group of well-groomed proud men from the area pose along with him at the putting green in Meenan's Park in the 1950s. Includes: Dan Feeney, Danny 'Glut' Doherty, J McCay, Jim Breslin, Paddy Stone, B Curran, John McGir, 'Covey' Robinson, 'Banks' McMenamin, J Phelan, Brendan Curran, John McGinley, Neil Boyle, Ronnie Lamberton, Patrick Ryan and Johnny McFadden. (Courtesy John McGinley.)

collars starched stiff. They put on the collars themselves in the morning by attaching them with bone-like button studs, and on quite a few Sunday mornings when one accidentally slipped from between my father's fumbling fingers, there was a whole commotion as we had to search for it on our hands and knees to find it under the dresser or kitchen table.

My father shaved himself with an open razor with a white bone handle that housed the sharp blade that folded into it like a penknife. The razor was sharpened by rubbing it from side to side on a thick broad leather strap that was attached by one end to a nail at the back of the door. On Sundays, everybody was to be kind and friendly, all quarrels put aside, and the King of Peace ruled and reigned. That's what we were taught as children and believed was the right way to behave.

Lent and Easter Chicks

During the six weeks of Lent, everyone went on a strict fast. Each day we had only one main meal consisting of two or three potatoes and a small piece of meat. Two other smaller meals were eaten of one or two rounds of bread and a cup or bowl of tea. No one went to the cinema, dancing was definitely forbidden and all the dance halls were closed for the duration. Apart from fasting, most people also undertook other forms of penance like staying off sugar, sweets, snuff and cigarette smoking – big sacrifices for people who at that time were living in poverty and hunger every day, but who were still very religious.

Easter Sunday was eagerly looked forward to at the end of Lent. We would all go to early Mass in the Long Tower and afterwards rush home for a feast of eggs – boiled, fried, poached or whatever way you wanted them. Only the very lucky families got chocolate and sweets, so most painted bright designs on hard-boiled eggs to the delight of their children. Some rolled their eggs down some nearby slope or hill to represent the rolling away of the stone from the tomb where Jesus arose from the dead on the first Easter morning.

Around Easter time every year, Freddie and I were each given sixpence to go to the hatcheries on Foyle Street to buy day-old chicks at

My sister Susie in the yard with cousin Bridget Lynch
holding Margaret in her arms (1940s).

a penny apiece. It was so exciting to bring home a dozen little fluffy
yellow cheeping birds in two cardboard boxes with the little air holes in
them. We were allowed to keep them in the house for a couple of days
until they were hardy enough to be put into the back yard. As they got
older, two or three of them might die, and the survivors, which usually
included a rooster, lived in a shed beside the coalhouse and the toilet,
and eventually some of them began to lay eggs.

It was exciting to run into the shed in the mornings and feel about
in the straw to find the lovely warm eggs. We loved to have them boiled

Dancing the night away at the ceilidh in the Corinthian Ballroom, Bishop St (1950s). (Courtesy Patricia Ward, Central Library.)

and put into an eggcup and have the top sliced off so we could guzzle them down for breakfast. Happy days! Sometimes, whenever we went out to the yard to the toilet, the rooster would peck at our bare legs, so we had to protect ourselves by swiping at it with the sweeping brush. After a while it got crafty and would jump onto the brush, so we had to drop it and run for safety.

Paddy Strain's Donkey and Pampered Chicks

On sunny days we played on the banking, and sometimes we would all sit up on Paddy Strain's back-yard wall, a height of seven feet, and look at all the smoking chimneys and rooftops down below in the Bogside. There would be about ten of us, including a few girls, all jostling for the best seats on the wall, and an odd time one of us would fall off, but we always landed without any serious injuries and just climbed up again to reclaim a good seat.

Paddy 'Gouldie' Carlin from Friel's Terrace with his niece Teeda McLaughlin, giving his donkey a tit-bit out of a white enamelled basin on the top of the banking in 1944. Below them is St Columb's Street and Wellington Street with the row of air raid shelters along the left hand side. (Courtesy Jimmy Doherty.)

One day Paddy Strain brought a donkey he had bought from a gypsy up the banking. He carried it across his shoulders and we watched him as he came up the steep slope from the direction of Fox's Corner. When he reached the top of the banking, he shouted to one of his sons to open the gate so that he could put the donkey into the back yard. He gave us all rides on it before doing so, and we made friends with it. The next day when we went to see it, the donkey was gone.

Paddy also bought a dozen young chicks one spring from the hatcheries in Foyle Street, and because they were so small, they had to be kept in the heat until they grew hardy enough to be put out into the yard. Paddy decided to put the chicks into the older children's bedroom and put the children's beds into the shed in the back yard where they had to sleep until the chickens were ready to be put outside and fattened for Christmas.

Halloween Rocket Scare

On Halloween, my father would burn a cork over the lighted gas and then spit on it to cool it. The blackened cork was rubbed on our faces to disguise us when we dressed up for Halloween night. We didn't go around the houses in those days, because people just hadn't got any surplus fruit or sweets to give away.

A neighbour's husband had just come home after working in England and he brought some fireworks with him for Halloween that couldn't be bought here. On Halloween night, the woman of the house invited us all into her front room for a party, as her husband was out having a drink in Devine's pub in Walker's Square. She took the fireworks out of the cupboard and told us to sit on the floor. We had never seen a firework before, and neither had the woman, so she read the instructions that said to light the blue touch paper at the bottom of the firework. She held the long stick that was attached to it and lit the blue paper. We all sat with our eyes wide open in amazement waiting to see the lovely coloured lights that were supposed to sparkle from the firework.

Suddenly, the rocket shot out of her hand with a jet of smoke and flame behind it and everyone in the room began to yell and scream as it flew round the room, bouncing off the walls and ceiling. Some of us managed to rush out the door and the rest huddled under the table with the neighbour. Everyone was crying their eyes out with fear. Whenever the whooshing noise stopped and the rocket had ended up embedded under the fire grate, we came out from under the table spluttering and coughing through the smoke and ran as fast as our legs could carry us out into the middle of the street. Luckily, no one came to any harm and we all had a great laugh about it later.

Christmas Preparations

November was the time of the year when we were encouraged to start saving our pennies and halfpennies for Christmas. My mother washed out empty syrup or treacle tins for Susie, Freddie and me to use as moneyboxes, and my father soldered a few spots around the edges of the lids to make them burglar-proof. Then a slot was made in the lids just wide enough to insert any coins given to us by my father or older members of the family.

Whenever any of our aunts or uncles visited the house, the moneyboxes were taken from their hiding places to be given a wee rattle in the hope that a few more precious pennies might be deposited. My Uncle Willie Cooley, who lived in the men's hostel in Charlotte Street, always ignored us and told my mother to put a bit of manners into us.

By the time Christmas week came, we had saved about six shillings each, and then it was time to empty the moneyboxes. We inserted the flat blade of a knife into the slot and turned the box upside down so that the coins slid along the blade and out through the slot. It took a bit of jiggling and fiddling for a few minutes until the last valuable halfpenny dropped out onto the table.

In the Brow of the Hill Christian Brothers' School, a couple of days before the Christmas holidays, schoolwork continued as usual until the last few hours when the lay teachers – Paddy Carlin, Tommy 'Nobby'

Paddy McCallion with his workers, standing outside his grocery shop and bar at 228-230 Bishop Street in the 1920s. (Courtesy Charley Logue.)

Carr, Gerry Stone and Barney Doherty – began to tidy up their presses and let us read our favourite books. However, some of the Christian Brothers teachers kept up their strict routines until the bell rang and the classes erupted in a stampede of happy excited pupils.

About a week before Christmas we used to get very excited and write on a piece of paper the things that we wished Santa Claus to put into our stockings that were hung at the foot of our beds on Christmas Eve. We would then put the notes to Santa above the lighted fire in the living room and the draught pulled them up the chimney. We thought Santa would find and read them whenever he came down our chimney early on Christmas morning.

Christmas trees or decorations were not put up then in the houses or shops and because there was no way to keep food fresh, the shopping wasn't done until Christmas Eve. The town centre bustled with people carrying shopping bags with little presents for their children's Christmas stockings. Plucked chickens and geese hung upside down, inside and outside the shop doorways; turkeys weren't a part of the Christmas fare then. The strong aromas of coffees and teas wafted out from the Maypole Tea and Coffee Blenders in Ferryquay Street. Returning Donegal expatriates, just off the Scotch and Liverpool boats, jostled through the shoppers in Foyle Street with packed suitcases to catch the buses and trains home to their families for Christmas.

In Christmas week, my mother made a large pudding mixed with fruits and spices, and also added a bottle of stout to the ingredients. The mixture was put into a pillowcase and steamed in a big pot over the fire for hours and the appetising aroma permeated the entire interior of the house. Aunt Julia also baked Christmas cakes, and to make the icing she mixed lard and sugar in a baking bowl and beat the mixture until it became soft enough to spread over the cakes. I loved to scoop the remnants of the mixture from the bowl with a spoon to eat.

Santa Claus was the big attraction in Woolworth's stores in Ferryquay Street the week before Christmas, and the children queued to see him as he jutted out of the makeshift chimney pot erected at the top of four wooden steps inside the store. To get a present when it was your turn, you had to hand him a shilling. He would then say: "Ho! Ho!

Ho!" as he gave you the gift wrapped in brown paper. I remember one Christmas when a boy in front of me didn't have a shilling for a present but, believing in the seasonal myths of joy and goodwill to all, handed Santa Claus a sixpenny piece instead. There was a moment's silence before Santa leaned over from his chimney pot and told the little boy, in a very unseasonable voice, to, "Eff off."

Christmas Celebrations

My father, at that time of the year, would invite some of his friends into the house for a drink of stout and a drop of whiskey. The same treat was given to the postman, the coalman, the milkman and the breadman, all of whom delivered their goods promptly the whole year round. As a result of this seasonal generosity, it wasn't unusual to see a horse plodding along pulling the cart containing its over-inebriated sleeping driver home at a late hour before Christmas.

The bottles of stout were bought in Willie Devine's public house in Walker's Square, and when the corks were pulled, the drink was poured into white delft bowls. After a while, when the top went off the stout, my father heated the poker in the fire and plunged it into the bowl to make the head creamy again. A couple of stouts later, the men would eventually begin to sing, and my father gave them a rendering of his favourite songs: *Just a Song at Twilight, When the Lights are Low* and *I Love Old Ireland Still*. His most favourite was *Oft in the Stilly Night*, and everyone sat quietly as he gently sang. It was so peaceful listening to them singing as I lay cosily tucked up in my bed before I drifted off to sleep.

The Naked Goose

One day, a woman in the street won a live goose at the Christmas rickety wheel in Our Lady of Lourdes Hall in the Brandywell and her husband had to bring it home, trussed up under his arm. However, he didn't know how to kill it properly and hadn't the heart to chop its head off, so he hit it with a hammer and then he and his wife plucked it and hung it up behind the scullery door. Half an hour later, it suddenly started to flap and honk and create a terrible commotion and had to be untied to run panicking around the room, naked! It looked so weird and ugly that none of the neighbours would approach it and the woman had to rush into the town to get a chicken for the Christmas dinner instead of having the goose. She got fond of the goose through time and knitted it a woollen cardigan to wear until its feathers grew back again. She kept it as a pet for a number of years and we fed it crusts of bread sometimes.

Pet Hen on the Menu

We each had a favourite chicken that we reared in the yard and Freddie got very fond of his pet hen that he called Jenny. One Christmas time, when we came in from school, Freddie ran out to the yard to see Jenny. He couldn't find her and came into the living room where Danny and I were standing staring up at the back of the door looking at Jenny and three other hens hanging from a hook, their feet tied up with cord and them plucked clean. Freddie cried his eyes out at the dinner table on Christmas Day when he saw the hens on the big roasting tin with their legs sticking up and the steam rising from them. He couldn't bring himself to eat his dinner on that particular Christmas day.

Christmas Eve and Stockings

On Christmas Eve night, we were bathed in the big tin bath in front of the fire. The clean clothes I was to wear at the Christmas morning Mass hung over the brass rail below the high mantelpiece: new short trousers, snake-buckle belt and gansey, my grey long-tailed shirt and grey woollen knee-length socks. Lined along the top of the fire fender were our polished black leather boots and my sister's patent leather shoes.

We got our bowls of porridge before scampering up to bed by candlelight and slipping under our blankets, fearful of being caught awake by Santa who might refuse to fill our empty stockings that hung at the foot of our beds. I thought about Ned McDevitt's two donkeys with the dark crosses on their backs and knew that at midnight, when we would be fast asleep, they would go down on their front knees to adore the Baby Jesus.

In the darkness of the early Christmas morning we awoke to search through our bulging stockings to find a variety of gifts: a colouring book, an apple and an orange, a threepenny bit and a toy gun or an aeroplane made from balsa wood. Small and insignificant presents compared to today's standards, but we still derived great pleasure from them.

"I wish our ma would hurry up with the towel because our bums are freezing."
Getting washed in the tin bath in front of the fire-range, watched by the two
wee spectators in the cot in the corner.

Christmas Mass and Dinner

A Snowflake
by Phil Cunningham

Where does it come from, where does it go?
I've questioned and pondered, does anyone know?
It lands on my roof, the ground and my nose.
I wonder who made it, this white flake of snow?

On Christmas morning we went to the school's ten o'clock Mass in the Long Tower Church where we sang the Nativity hymns *Adeste Fideles* and *Hark the Herald Angels Sing* among others of the period. One Christmas morning there was a covering of snow on the rooftops and ground, even the statue of Governor Walker was white on one side. The bells of St Columb's Cathedral were joyously pealing out over the Walls, and St Eugene's Cathedral bells chimed from the opposite height above the Bogside. Even then, on that Christmas morning, it sounded as if they were attempting to exchange greetings across the calm peaceful void above our houses on the back of the Walls.

The Christmas dinner at midday consisted of soup, potatoes, peas, chicken and gravy. Then we got a dish of lovely jelly and custard to finish it all off. Before my mother boiled the potatoes, she put them in a large tin bucket that she placed under the water tap in the back yard and Freddie or me had to swish them around in the water with the shaft of the brush to get the clay off them. When the potatoes were boiled, we mashed them with a wooden beetle, shaped like a thick wooden table leg, and when the spuds were pounded, Aunt Julia would say, "I hope there are no juke-the-beetles amongst those poundies." That meant she hoped we hadn't missed any little pieces of potato when we were mashing them.

There were usually sixteen or seventeen for dinner so the eight younger ones ate first and then the others, a busy morning for my mother, Aunt Julia and the older girls because the men didn't do any kind of cooking or housework. After dinner, we played the popular board games of Ludo, Snakes and Ladders, and Tiddlywinks, which we all enjoyed. In the late evening, our Uncle Joe Cooley and his wife

Rosie from Bishop Street visited us with their family and then it was time to eat the iced cake and buns with big glasses of lemonade and play more games with our cousins. I didn't know until I got a bit older that Rosie was my father's niece and Uncle Joe was my mother's brother, so I stopped calling her my Aunt Rosie because she was really my cousin Rosie.

Boxing Day Leftovers and Football

On Boxing Day, the younger members of the household were up early whilst the older ones, who had gone to their beds a lot later than usual, were still sleeping. I got dressed and Freddie, Danny and I ate a piece of Christmas pudding and an iced bun that had survived from the Christmas tea for our breakfasts. All that was left of the Christmas dinner chickens were the bones that were now in the big pot hanging from the black bar on a hook above the dead fire. It was filled with vegetables and water, ready from the night before to be made into soup for the day's dinner.

Out on the street and on the banking, all was quiet and peaceful except for the chirping of the sparrows on the Walls and under the eaves. Nearly everyone in the streets below in the Bogside must have been still in their beds too because only an odd chimney pot here and there was beginning to smoke from a newly kindled fire in the grate. Johnny McDermott's white horse and Ned McDevitt's two donkeys were contentedly grazing at the bottom of the banking behind the band shed.

Later in the day, after our dinners of soup and spuds, my father took us to the Brandywell football grounds to watch Derry City in their black and white colours playing a friendly match with a team selected from other local football outfits. There were always huge crowds and on our way into the grounds, my father lifted us over the turnstile. We played about most of the time and could always hear the loudest man, Danny McDaid of Nailor's Row, shouting above the crowd. Hawker Lynch also kept everyone amused with his witty remarks whilst his sidekick, Johnny 'Cuttems' McLaughlin, chased the other young boys and me off the greyhound track that ran alongside the pitch.

A section of the spectators watching Derry City playing in the Brandywell in 1935. The well-known Hawker Lynch is sitting at the front on the extreme left. (Courtesy David Bigger collection.)

Crazy Chimps

Do you mind last night, the night before?
Three wee monkeys came to the door.
One had a fiddle, one had a drum,
And the other had a pancake stuck to his bum.

Every year the circus came to town and set up their big top in the cattle market at the rear of Fahan Street and Rossville Street. One year there was great excitement when four of the chimpanzees escaped and climbed onto the roofs of the houses at the top of Waterloo Street and Fahan Street. I ran down with my pals to join the crowd of spectators gathered at Butcher's Gate to watch the antics of the monkeys.

The chimps climbed up onto the chimney stacks and began to swing from the pots. The more curious monkeys started to investigate the insides of the chimney pots and were immediately covered in smoke that poured out around their faces. It was amusing to see them dancing about screaming and beating their hands against the pots in fear and anger.

But one monkey wasn't content just to get smoke damaged, as a group of local musicians found out.

The McCallion family lived in Fahan Street at that time and they had a vacant attic which none of the family ever entered because the old granny always warned the youngsters that it was haunted. A few men from the area, among them 'Oakey' Ramsey, Johnny Steel and John McCallion (from another family), were starting a ceilidh band so they had rented the attic room for practising in and ignored the warning from Granny McCallion about it being haunted by a human-like creature. The band members were practising in the attic that particular evening when they heard tapping on the skylight. On looking up, they saw to their horror a hairy shape trying to open the window. The men bolted for the door and tumbled down the stairs in fright. It turned out to be one of the escaped circus monkeys still on the roof who obviously had an ear for music and wanted to join the ceilidh. He certainly made a reel of the bandsmen anyway!

The monkeys were free for most of the day until their handlers coaxed them down off the roofs with food just before dusk. Some people said that the escapes were arranged deliberately to publicise the arrival of the circus in town.

Homework and Rats

I sometimes did my homework on the broad inside sill of the landing window because it was quiet and bright with the western light. I was also able to look down into our backyard to watch the hens pecking at the scraps of food in the big tin basin that was always left out for them. One evening when I looked down into the yard, I saw four big rats eating out of the hen's basin. When I tapped on the windowpane, they darted into the coalhouse where my father kept two greyhounds in an elevated kennel above the coal which the dogs got into by walking up a plank.

Later that day, when my father and Willie came in for a tea break, as they usually did when they were working in the area, a rat scurried into the house straight past them. They slammed the door to keep it from escaping and then chased it around the room with brooms. Unfortunately, in the excitement of the chase, Willie hit my father on the back of the head with the brush and he swore at Willie. They created a terrible racket and in the confusion and the swearing the rat made good its escape somehow or other.

When I was very young, I slept in the downstairs front room at the foot of my father and mother's bed. After I was put to bed one night, a rat climbed up the back of the bed and clung onto my hair behind my pillow. Nobody believed me when I told them about it next day, and they said that I must have been dreaming. Later on that year, Mickey laid poison for them when we had no hens, and got thirteen dead rats under the dog kennel in the shed.

Doggy Yarns and Races

My father's greyhounds had to be exercised every day and sometimes he walked them with Danny, Freddie and I up Bligh's Lane and into the fields that were later to become part of Creggan. I loved to slip off their leads and let them race around, admiring their natural speed as they chased each other up and down. When we got home again, we rubbed their muscles with liniment oil to keep them fit. Then we fed them and put them into the kennel.

I remember taking them a walk one morning up the Watery Lane above the city cemetery to a pond where we used to catch sticklebacks. It was known as the Doctor's Dam and was noted to be a dangerous place for children to play. I tied the greyhounds to a whinbush by their leads and began fishing, using a stick with a piece of thread and a small worm tied to it. But my luck was out because my Uncle Eddie Cooley passed by and spotted me and later told my father. The Derry Walls were the only place I was allowed to walk the dogs around after that for a month.

To make up for visiting the forbidden Doctor's Dam, I decided to walk the dogs for my father very early one sunny Saturday morning. I rose at six o'clock, got dressed, quietly took the dogs out of their kennel, put their leads on and headed out. It was a beautiful June morning and the hundreds of sparrows that nested under the eaves and in nooks and crannies in Derry's Walls were making a loud din as they squabbled and quarrelled and chirped all at the same time. I was very happy thinking to myself how pleased my father would be to hear that the dogs had been given a good walk. I hoped he would take me and Freddie to the Brandywell dog track to see them racing; maybe even to cheer one of them coming in first past the finishing post. I had never been to a dog race there before, and hoped to see them compete some day, after all the walking and massaging that I had given them.

As I walked the greyhounds along the top of the banking, a huge marmalade coloured cat darted out from behind Johnny McDermott's shed, just about a foot in front of the brown dog on my left, and ran between my legs. Quick as a flash, the big black and white dog on my right hand made a snap at the cat and caught it by its hindquarters. It

'Budgim' Doherty
and 'Soots' Breslin
having a 'doggy chat'
at the junction of
Rossville Street, Fox's
Corner and the
Bogside in 1955.

began screeching and spitting, and then the other dog suddenly
clamped its jaws on the back of its neck. I was terrified as I tried to pull
the animals apart, with the poor cat trying to claw at the dogs as it
suffered a cruel death.

I was very upset and took the greyhounds back to their kennel with
blood streaming from the deep scratches on the black and white dog's
muzzle. I was glad my father wasn't angry when I explained what had
happened. I was even gladder when he said he would take us to see the
dogs racing at the Brandywell because they had had a kill and that
would make them hungry for another one at the racetrack. In those
days, the greyhound owners released young rabbits for their dogs to
chase and kill to give them a taste for blood so they would be eager to
catch the hare whenever they raced at the dog track.

There was another greyhound racing track in a field at Bligh's Lane
before Creggan Estate was built and my father and Johnny McGill took
us there to see some of the races. It was not as good as the Brandywell
because it was in the middle of a field full of rushes and the only shelter
available whenever it rained was under the thick hawthorn hedges.

Jock the Female Dog and Local 'Vets'

Bob Moore and his wife lived two houses up the street from us and had a Scotch terrier dog called Jock. We sometimes took it to the banking for him to give it some exercise. When we were looking after it one day, another strange dog came running up the slope and started to play with Jock. We tried to chase the dog away but it started to growl at us and scared us back a distance. Then it tried to climb onto Jock's back and we ran to get help from some neighbours in the street. When some women came along with us to see what was happening, the two dogs were just standing with their back ends together looking very sad. I thought their tails had become stuck with mud or tar and couldn't be separated.

The women began to call the dogs bad names and one woman got a bucket of water and threw it over them. Then another woman began screaming at them and beat them with a brush. She then pushed the dogs, still stuck together, over the edge of the banking and they rolled and tumbled and yelped in pain to the bottom where they separated and ran in opposite directions. Some months later, Jock had a litter of nice puppies and Bob just lifted the manhole lid in his yard and dropped them down into it. That's what happened in those days to unwanted litters of cats and dogs.

Dog owners were very particular about the length of their dog's tail, even though some of the animals were mongrels and were allowed to roam about the streets unchecked. In Derry, there were a few men who knew all about dogs but who weren't qualified vets. Any dog owner who needed to have their dog's tail shortened took it to be docked when it was only a week or two old; any older and the operation would have been too painful for the dog. The tails were just clipped off with a pair of scissors or a sharp knife and it was common knowledge that at least two of the 'vets' bit off the puppies' tails saying that it was less painful and more hygienic for the dog. Collie dogs and greyhounds were the only dogs to be seen with full tails in those times.

Buttermilk and Carts

"Where is my nose bag, I'm starving?" An Old City Dairy milk float and milkmen in the 1940s. (Courtesy John McCloskey.)

Every Saturday, the buttermilk carts came into Derry from Donegal. When the horse-drawn cart came into our street, the women queued up to fill their tin cans and jugs with buttermilk and to buy a pound or two of home-made country butter. The buttermilk tasted delicious and my mother or Julia used it when making scone bread.

I learned in later years that those drivers and horses were on the roads to Derry from two and three o'clock in the morning in order to sell their buttermilk, eggs and butter. As butter was rationed during the war, the only person in our household to have it on his bread was my father whenever it was available. Margarine was eaten most of the time and whenever it was scarce, people melted suet, which was a solid piece of animal fat. When the suet cooled down, it was poured into a jam jar and then used for spreading like butter on the bread or to fry with in the pan.

The bread vans were horse drawn, as were the coal carts, and in the early mornings the clip clop of the milkman's horse and the clinking of the milk bottles echoed off Derry's Walls as his cart came into the street. Our milkman was Jim Gillespie who also owned a bar on Duke Street in the Waterside. Hugh Gillen from Union Street, and his son Willie, delivered our coal.

The Henry family, who lived up the street in one of the six smaller houses in Nailor's Row, owned a pony and trap and went to all the fairs that were held in the outlying towns. They were also the only family in the area to own a motorcar. It was a big black one with high round mudguards and headlights sticking up at the front. The windows were tinted a dark amber and it had side running boards to stand on to get in or out. It was used as a taxi, and one day we went to Rathmullan in it, a long journey of thirty or forty miles in those times, to visit our mother's cousins.

Old Mrs Henry sold toffee apples and paper pokes of toffee popcorn for a penny, and sometimes we would find a dead cockroach stuck in the toffee. Of course, we just poked it out and ate our popcorn. Nowadays, people would probably try to sue for mental distress or something if they found a dead bug in their food but nobody bothered much then.

The Surprise Packet

Tillie Goode and her husband Dick, who was an officer in the British army, lived beside us with their three boys and three girls. One of the boys, Billy, was a bit older than the rest of us. He was good fun to play with and would march us younger boys around the banking and give us orders as if we were soldiers. Because he was older, Billy considered himself to be the leader of the gang and at times thought he had to prove it, as happened once with a new arrival in the street, George Stevenson, whose family had just moved in a couple of months previously.

One day, Billy had tried to show George just who was the boss by trying to goad him into a fight but his ploy didn't work because George just ignored him. To get his revenge, Billy handed Freddie a small brown paper parcel and said to him, "Take this up to George Stevenson, and tell him that I sent him these stripes." This was his way of saying he was the general and he was awarding military stripes to his underlings. Freddie, following his orders, knocked on George's door and when he answered, handed over the parcel and delivered the message. Unfortunately for Freddie, he was still at the door when George opened it because he immediately gave him a clout on the ear. Inside the parcel had been a big lump of dung and George wasn't very happy to receive it.

The Drowning of Cathal

In party mood in Nailor's Row in 1948 are the Stevensons, Fergusons and the Feeneys, with my friend Cathal on the extreme left. Joanna Logue and Cissie Diamond are in the back row. (Courtesy Andy Stevenson.)

The Stevenson family had moved into Nailor's Row from the Lone Moor Road. Cathal Stevenson, a boy of my age who was modest and shy and much taller than me, became one of my closest and best friends. Because the Lone Moor Road was virtually in the countryside in those days, Cathal had learned about animals and nature and was nicknamed 'Magwah' because he slightly resembled an American Indian who appeared in the Western cowboy films. He took us out into the fields and taught us all about birds and showed us how to look for their nests, and how not to damage them or any eggs or newly hatched chicks. I spent many long and happy summer days with

Cathal, rambling through the fields and walking the roads to climb Holywell Hill to gather blackberries and bilberries, and catching stickle backs and frogs. Cathal was always there to teach us and to protect us when we felt we were in any danger from bullies or from anything else that would do us any harm.

We always felt safe when we were with Cathal who had taken us out of the dusty smoky streets and away from the dirty crumbling buildings to the fresh clean air of the fields and trees in the countryside. Sadly, Cathal was to drown so tragically a few years later when we were all away together on an outing to Fahan, County Donegal.

On that fateful day, we were all about to board the bus to go home when someone called to Cathal to give him a hand to push a boat into Lough Swilly. Cathal obliged but for some reason, jumped into the boat when it was afloat. One of the boys then pushed the boat out into the deeper water. Someone shouted to Cathal to jump out while it was still in the shallows but Cathal didn't want to get his trousers wet.

Unknown to us, the boat was in bad condition and it suddenly started leaking. None of us could swim, so Mickey Rush waded out as far as he could and pushed an oar out to Cathal but it drifted past the boat. We watched helplessly as Cathal tried to bail out the water with his hands but to no avail. The boat filled rapidly and overturned. Cathal was thrown into the Lough and started to splash frantically and cry out for help. It was all over in a matter of a few short minutes and the empty boat drifted back in again upside down. I was horrified and felt as though a black cloth had suddenly been put around my brain. I sat down on the roadside with my hands tightly wrapped around the top of my head, trying to keep out the reality of the scenes I had just witnessed.

I couldn't believe what had happened. My friend Cathal, whom I had loved and respected, was gone forever, never again to roam with us along the road to Holywell Hill or through the fields. That happened in May 1952 when we were teenagers and two years after I had left the back of the Walls.

There were other people on the shore that day who thought that we were all having a bit of boisterous fun, including three Royal Navy sailors on a day trip to Fahan. A woman who was watching from her house that overlooked the Lough, came out to her front garden and waved a white tablecloth as a signal for help to the Browns who lived across the Fahan creek on Inch Island. Two of the Browns were skilled boatmen, and on seeing the signal, launched a boat that reached the scene of the accident within minutes, but they were too late to save our friend Cathal.

Two other acquaintances were drowned in Lough Swilly at Fahan shortly after in the same year. One was Daniel McMonagle from Long Tower Street who had helped to carry Cathal's coffin only the previous month. Daniel took a cramp while learning to swim at the pier. The other was a young lad called Raymond Sharkey from the Strand Road who was wading along with his girlfriend in shallow water at low tide. He stepped into the deep channel out of his depth and was swept away.

Fahan Shore
(To Cathal)

*Gentle ripples are lapping the shore where an upturned
    boat basks in the warm May sun.*
*Then happy teenage sounds upset the pleasant scene as they
    play and search for boisterous fun.*
*"Upturn the boat," one calls and eager, soft hands obey as
    sand and seaweed scatter about the scrum.*
*Away, me Hearties, the boat is launched on the outgoing
    tide against an evening setting sun*
While a dark danger rushed from a gaping hole.
They flee and one boy is left, afraid to run.
*Gentle ripples are lapping the shore where an upturned
    boat basks, its deed being done.*
*When the sea spewed through its rotting plank to swamp
    and take the laughing, crying one.*

Nelson Street after the close of the men's annual retreat mission. Some are wearing the customary retreat white flower on their coat lapel. (Courtesy Rev B Canning.)

Collapsing Toilets and the Oaks Hall

If Governor Walker happened to fall,
He would kill all the people on the back of the Wall.

When I was out in the back yard washing my hands one day, I heard a heavy rumbling noise. It sounded like close thunder, and I thought that Walker's Pillar had fallen down. I looked up to check and there he was, with his arm outstretched, still pointing towards the River Foyle. I ran to the street to find out what had happened and learned that the back yards and toilets of some of the houses on lower Nailor's Row had collapsed and fallen down the banking to the back of Fahan Street.

There were about ten families including the O'Briens, MacNamees, Bridges and the Deans living in the houses and some of them were moved to an old abandoned fever hospital on Foyle Hill. The rest were re-housed in prefabricated aluminium bungalows on Anne Street in the Brandywell.

Danny Moore lived in the biggest house at the back of the Walls. It was three storeys high and adjoined the top of Friel's Terrace and Nailor's Row. The house was previously a school and behind it, on the top of the banking, was a small cottage with a flower and vegetable garden where the schoolteacher had once lived. An old lady named Annie Diven, now stayed there with her daughter. Annie wore long black skirts to her ankles and a black shawl around her shoulders. I only ever saw her poking about in her garden when I peeped in through her hedge as I played on the banking.

Danny was a foreman in the shipyard on Derry's quay and he and Dan Feeney, who also worked in the shipyard, built a rowing boat in the corrugated tin shed called the Oaks Dance Hall behind our house. I remember looking in at them sawing and planing the wood, and then seeing the boat being taken away on a trailer to be launched on the River Foyle.

About a year later, we heard loud hammering noises coming from behind the street and ran around to the backs of the houses to investigate. There was a group of men dismantling the Oaks Hall and the mice and rats were darting about in every direction. We had great fun chasing and throwing stones at them. After the Hall was demolished, we poked through the dust and debris for hours finding coins of every value that had fallen through the seams and cracks in the floorboards over the years. Our pockets were jingling for a few days afterwards.

As well as the Oaks Hall behind our house, there was the Emmet's Hall on the banking behind Walker's Square at the end of Howard's Place. The hall was named after Robert Emmet, one of the leaders of the failed 1798 Irish uprising who was publicly hanged, drawn and quartered in Dublin. It was knocked down when I was five but I remember hearing the sounds of music coming from it as ceilidhs were often held there.

Fishing and Dickie Valley

When we got a bit older, about eight or nine, we began fishing down at Derry docks. For fishing line, we used about fifty feet of whipcord and two feet of catgut, as they called it then. Catgut was also used for tennis racquet strings and the horse and cart drivers used the cord to pleat their horsewhips. We baited the hook with a bit of fish or a worm, tied a piece of lead above the gut, and cast into the muddy swirling river behind the Strand Road to catch dab fish or fluke. Fluke were flat fish and when it was time to go home, we had about five each. I took mine home to my mother who fried them over the open fire and they tasted lovely to a very hungry boy. We fished there for a couple of years and always took the catch home to eat until someone pointed out to us that we were fishing at a spot where the sewers emptied the waste into the river. We decided then to do our fishing away down below the dry dock near Pennyburn in cleaner water.

One day, as we were walking along the wharf beside the river, a young thin man took off all his clothes, except his grey underpants, and jumped into the river. He quickly sank and we couldn't see him surfacing. Some dockers were passing by and, thinking that the man had drowned, we quickly told them what had happened. When we described the man to them, they all began to laugh. They told us not to worry about him because the same man took a swim in the river every day and that he was called Dickie Valley from Bridge Street. Sure enough they were right because when we looked down the river, Dickie was climbing up a ladder onto the quay about fifty yards away, near to where the Liverpool and Scotch boats were docked.

Nearly Strangled

One Sunday afternoon, Freddie, John Reid and I went up the Bogside intending to go to Brooke Park. Sunday evenings were always very quiet on the streets because people went out into the country for a walk and many went to bed to read the Sunday papers and have a snooze. We were only about six or seven years old at the time, and as we walked along chatting we were joined by a bigger boy of about twenty. He told us he knew where a cave was nearby and that he would take us to it. Freddie and John didn't want to go but I was eager for the adventure so I went along with him. We went down a street at the top of the Bogside and over a back lane behind a big red bricked building where we crawled in through a small hole at ground level. It was pitch dark inside and we were stumbling over piles of bricks and rubble. There was water running somewhere inside in the creepy darkness, and I became very scared of the blackness and the echoing sounds and told the man I wanted to go home with my pals.

He told me to be quiet and then I felt his hands and fingers around my throat. I could feel his breath on the side of my face and I began to scream and wriggle about. Then I grabbed his wrists as he tightened his grip on my windpipe and we both stumbled on the loose bricks. I broke free and scrambled towards the small beam of light that was my escape hole out of the cave and back into the quiet sunny Sunday afternoon.

After escaping, I met my brother Freddie and John Reid who had decided to wait for me at the top of the Bogside. I told them everything that had happened to me and warned them not to tell anyone else in case I would get into trouble with my mother and father. However, they must have told because I learned a few weeks later that my older brothers, Paddy, Willie and Mickey, settled the score with the man who had nearly strangled me. They were always very kind and protective to the rest of us and we loved them very much.

The Stagecoach

The Feeney family lived in number six; they had three sons and three daughters. One son, John, known as Danno, was a good footballer and played for Glentoran and Derry. His younger brother Dan was a very jovial person and drove a horse-drawn coach for the local undertaker. It was black and shining with a lantern mounted on either side of the high driver's seat. Two big shining black horses with large black feather plumes attached to the top of their heads pulled the passenger coach, and another pair of grand horses drew the four-wheeled glass-sided black hearse.

At my Granda Cunningham's funeral, all the youngest grandsons travelled in the coach because in those days the older boys and men walked to the cemetery and no females went to the burial. Dan was driving the coach and when it passed the Brandywell football ground, he stood up from his driving seat to look over the wall to see the match in progress.

Another day when we were coming from my granny's funeral, Dan pretended to us he was driving the stagecoach as in the cowboy movies. We pretended to shoot out at the Indians and Dan was shooting too as the horses galloped along the Lone Moor Road and through the Brandywell to the Lecky Road where my granny had lived. It was great fun for us but Dan's behaviour got him sacked and he then got a job in the hospital as a porter. He came in from work one day and his mother asked him for a match to light the fire. When she opened the matchbox, there was a finger in it that Dan had brought home from his work. She began to scream and ran out into the front street and fainted.

Feeding Time and Unexpected Contacts

Most newly born babies in those days were breast-fed and it was not unusual on a summer day to see a mother sitting on her front doorstep feeding her baby. But most mothers were more private about the practice and I can't say I ever noticed it in my own home.

The innocence of the times can be seen in the occasion when a woman sitting on her doorstep was trying to breast-feed her baby but with little success. Just then, a stranger who happened to be passing by heard her say to the baby, "If you don't take it, I will give it to that nice man over there." It was the innocent ways of the people that made the locality a peaceful and safe area to live in.

The First Derry Presbyterian Church School was just inside Derry's Walls at the bottom of Stable Lane. On holy days, when we were off school, we could hear the noises of the First Derry children as they played outside during their lunch break. Sometimes one or two of them peeped over the Walls and we waved up to them, and sometimes they waved back and then quickly disappeared. That was the only contact we ever had with the Protestant school children.

One day a man and a woman were looking down at us playing in the street, and they had a little boy with them. They stood him on the top of the Walls to watch us playing, and he fell down into Nailor's Row. He just lay there on the ground and didn't even cry because he must have been unconscious. Bobby Henry lifted him and carried him up around through Bishop's Gate to the parents who were coming to meet him from the Walls. We never knew what happened to him after that or even if he was badly injured.

Local beauty, Angela O'Doherty, at Bishop's Gate in the 1960s. (Courtesy Willie Carson collection.)

The Twelfth of August

We'll shout out, "No Surrender."
We'll come when duty calls.
With heart in hand and gallant band,
We'll guard old Derry's Walls.

The Twelfth of August was a big day for the Protestant residents living in the nearby Fountain. That was when they celebrated the relief of Derry from the 1689 siege. On the eleventh night, they lit a huge bonfire in the Fountain area and we younger boys went there to enjoy all the carry on. The adults stood around in small groups laughing and talking, and the sounds of music and rousing songs drifted out into the streets from Willie Martin's bar in London Street and Joe Kelly's bar in

Festivities on 11 August in the Fountain Estate in the 1950s. (Courtesy Leo Coyle.)

Celebration parade by the Apprentice Boys of Derry on the Walls on 12 August 1954. (Courtesy Rev B Canning.)

74

Wapping Lane. Even though we were known to have come from the back of the Walls area, we were never made to feel unwelcome, nor did we feel to be in any danger. But we might have had a different impression if we had stayed until the bars emptied at the official time of half past ten instead of going home early to our beds.

In those days in Derry, people of both religions moved about and mingled with each other in the cinemas and dance halls in safety. They even packed into the Brandywell to cheer on their local team, Derry City FC. As children, we were unaware of the religious divisions, politics, traditions or cultures that existed. I had even seen on the Twelfth, sash-bedecked Orangemen and their wives sitting on the footpaths in Fahan Street, resting their feet, and the women taking picnics from their baskets. They had their black bowler hats sitting beside them and there was never any physical harm directed at them, just a few funny remarks from the locals who stood at Fox's Corner. Not until I was much older did I learn that a few families in our areas had Protestant relations living in the Fountain Street region, but, as children, it made no difference to us.

Band Music and Scruffy Boys

The first music I ever heard was from the bands playing on the Walls every Twelfth of August parade. Dozens of bands marched along the Walls with thousands of Orangemen in black bowler hats and sashes around their necks waving Orange Lodge banners. The drums would pound and the bands would play *The Sash, Derry's Walls, Dolly's Brae* and many other tunes. We were not allowed to look out of our bedroom windows that faced the Walls in case some vandals would throw stones at us, as had happened before to our houses in other years.

I was born on the tenth of August and christened on the Twelfth. My Aunt Maggie took me to the Long Tower Church to be christened and jokingly claimed the bands were playing for me as she carried me up the street to the church.

At the age of seven or eight, my pals and I began to venture in through Butcher's Gate and onto the Walls. One Twelfth of August,

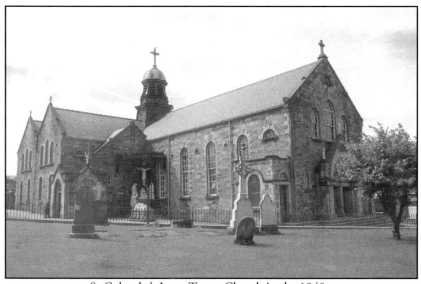

St Columba's Long Tower Church in the 1940s.
(Courtesy Willie Carson collection.)

Hill's shop on the corner of Asylum Road and Strand Road, decorated
for a royal occasion in the 1930s. (Courtesy Nan Hill.)

The Doherty brothers, James and George, putting up the shutters in Friel's Terrace for the Twelfth of August in the 1950s. (Courtesy Jimmy Doherty.)

when the Apprentice Boys parade was taking place, we joined the crowds that were assembled outside the Memorial Hall. There were long tables on the street laden with glasses of lemonade and biscuits and sandwiches, free to anyone who wished to partake. We were all happily scoffing away, enjoying the occasion, when two big hefty bowler-hatted Orangemen approached us and asked us where we lived. When we told them we came from the back of the Walls, they told us to run away home like good little boys, "for your mothers might be looking for youse." In our innocence, we hadn't realised that because we had been playing about on the streets all morning before we went up to the parade, we were a bit scruffy looking and weren't suitably attired for the occasion.

We used to like listening to the bands, and I especially liked to hear the accordions; they sounded so melodious. We had no radio or any

Society Street in the 1940s with the Apprentice Boys' Memorial Hall on the left.

musical instruments in our house until later years, so except for the church organ and bells, the Orange bands were the first live music we had ever heard. When we were a little older, we had lessons from Johnny McBride who taught bagpipe music in one of the house cellars on Fahan Street. He led a band called the 'Pride of Erin' which wasn't allowed to play inside the city Walls because it was a nationalist band and played Irish tunes. Johnny McBride's Pride of Erin band could only play in and around the nationalist Brandywell and Bogside areas.

On St Patrick's Day 1953, I was in the crowd when the band marched down Shipquay Street and the police confiscated the Irish and American flags at the head of it. Then they arrested some of the participants, causing a riot that lasted until midnight. The whole town was at a standstill and even the dockers stopped work and marched to the Strand Road police station with their coal shovels on their shoulders to protest about some of their workmates being arrested.

Sammy and the Big Day

Sure it's on the Twelfth, I will dress myself
With the sash my father wore.

Sammy Ferguson was a Belfast man who had met and married a Derry girl from the area and had settled in Nailor's Row. Their oldest son was about fifteen years old and every year, near the Twelfth of July and the Twelfth of August, Sammy took his son to visit his cousins in Belfast for a few days.

One August Twelfth, Sammy's wife decided to go up to the Diamond to see the bands and as she watched, she couldn't believe her eyes when, behind a Belfast banner as proud as punch in full Orange regalia, came marching her son and her husband. She raised a whole commotion when she broke through the ranks, grabbed her son, and took him down to the house with Sammy and a few Orangemen pleading with her to let him finish the walk. She discovered later that they had being marching for the past few years. She soon put an end to that and Sammy nearly got his final marching orders, this time from his wife.

Lundy Burning

Colonel Robert Lundy's name has become associated with treachery in Derry. Lundy was the Governor during the siege of Derry in 1689 who was forced to flee the city because the besieged citizens believed he was going to sell them out to the enemy, King James. They claimed he sold the keys of the Gates of Derry for a bap to aid his escape. Lundy fled to Scotland where he was arrested for treason though never actually tried. He eventually made his way to Europe and later become a high-ranking officer in the Portuguese army before his death in 1717.

Effigy of Lundy. (Courtesy Tower Museum.)

The Protestant Apprentice Boys of Derry association used to burn an effigy of Lundy 'The Traitor' on the eighteenth of December every year from Walker's Pillar on the Walls until it was blown up in 1973. They would hang him from the monument during the night, and in the morning, fire three blank shots from a cannon on the Walls as part of the ceremony.

Very early one dark December morning, Freddie and I were abruptly woken by the reports from the cannon. We got up and ran down the street in our bare feet to look up at Lundy hanging from the pillar. His big black coat was fluttering in the wind and his big black boots were shining in the moonlight. He wore a huge admiral's hat and had a bundle of sticks tied to his back. As we stared up at him, the wind swung him around to face us, then a voice shouted down: "Get away up to the house and get your boots on." We were terrified, and scampered up home again like scared mice and jumped into our bed, pulling the blankets over our heads. We thought Lundy had spoken to us, and by the end of the day, the whole street was talking and laughing about the incident.

In the evenings, when Lundy was to be burned, some people in our area stuffed lighted newspapers up their chimneys to burn the soot in the hope that the wind would blow the black smoke onto the Walls where the Apprentice Boys would be assembled. A couple of weeks later, some of the residents were made to pay a fine of about two shillings in the courthouse for daring to annoy the Boys by making more smoke than Lundy the Traitor. Mrs Ramsey, in Walker's Square, was one of the last people I remember getting fined for burning her chimney in the early 1940s. It was a very rare occasion when the wind blew in the desired direction, and the black smoke usually drifted harmlessly up into the sky and over the Bogside.

We all gathered on lower Nailor's Row outside Minnie Boyle's small front-room shop to watch in awe and fear Lundy blazing and crackling on the pillar. We could feel the heat from the flames, and often fireworks packed inside the effigy would explode, scaring the younger children and making them hide their faces in their mother's aprons or run home scared. After the fire petered out, all that was left hanging on the pillar were the soles of Lundy's boots at the bottom of his wire frame and a black scorch mark up the monument to just below the statue of Governor Walker.

When the pillar was blown up in 1973 there were only one or two families living in Friel's Terrace then, along with my cousins, the Cooley family, who moved into number two after we left to go to Creggan.

Recycling

In those days, we could run about the banking in our bare feet without any fear of injury because no one discarded empty bottles or tins. Bottles were all returned to the shop for a refund of the deposit paid on purchase. Canned food was not sold then, except for tins of treacle and syrup which, when empty, were used to store other items. Nothing was thrown out; wood was used for fuel and kindling, and the *Derry Journal* and the *Belfast Telegraph* newspapers were used to light the fire or cut up into squares and hung up, with a cord through them, in the toilet. Not exactly artwork but practical.

Even empty orange boxes had their uses; when one was stood on its end, a piece of linoleum was nailed onto the top and a little curtain

"You are my big dote." J Deeney Brown with baby Bernadette beside a Jones and Lowther laundry van in Bishop Street in the 1940s. (Courtesy Margaret Brown.)

hung over the front to transform it into a handy bedside locker. Tea chests were great for storing bedclothes, delft and crockery but empty flour sacks were probably the most versatile item and could be recycled lots of ways in the home. They were made from white cotton and when my mother and Aunt Julia washed and bleached the print out of them, they made great sheets, aprons, pillowcases, curtains and nightdresses.

When the sheets began to wear in the middle, they cut out the thin parts and sewed a new flour bag piece into the centre. The thin pieces were then used as dish cloths and babies' nappies. Some handy women could make boys' shirts from the bleached sacks and sometimes, if the print hadn't been fully removed, it was funny to see some poor children running around with some lettering or the weight of the original bag – 140lbs – still visible across their back.

Pawnshops, Rags and Mud Money

There were three pawnshops near us: Crossan's on Rossville Street at the bottom of Fox's Corner; Arthur's near the top of Long Tower Street; and Barr's on Bishop Street between the jail and the Fountain. Above the door of a pawnshop hung their trading sign, three brass balls in the form of a triangle, two at the top and one at the bottom. People said that it meant two-to-one odds against you not getting your goods back again.

The pawnshop was a lifesaver for many families during the nineteen thirties, forties and fifties, and helped to pay the rent man and keep hunger outside the door. People got loans in lieu of any household item: shoes, clocks, ornaments, suits of clothes and bedclothes. Articles were usually pawned on a Monday morning, and on a Friday there would be a queue of people collecting their good shoes and clothes for the weekend, especially for going to church and Sunday Mass. The loans were repaid with a small extra charge added and most were usually from five shillings to about five pounds.

The pawnbroker got so familiar seeing the same people week in and week out that he didn't even bother opening some of the brown paper parcels they deposited, so some people would take a chance and substitute old rags and the like instead of the pledged articles. If the goods weren't collected within three months, they would be put on display in the pawnbroker's window to be sold. You can imagine his language when he opened one of the dodgey parcels that were not collected inside the redeemable time.

A little girl carrying a bundle out of Barr's Pawnshop beside Carroll's Bar in Rossville Street in the 1950s.

Locals go about their daily business outside Crossan's Pawnshop at the bottom of Fox's Corner on Rossville Street. Late 1940s.

The Pawnshop Man
by Phil Cunningham

A very brave man is the pawnshop man,
    to loan out lots of dough
For shoes and clocks and Sunday suits
    and every thing that goes.
There's a big long queue on a Monday,
    each one with a big brown packet
And Nellie Black has her radio back, Joe
    Deane his old tweed jacket.

Me mother sent me in one day with my
    father's watch and chain,
I lost the ticket coming home and they
    were never seen again.
When me Da came in and he found out,
    I got a hiding and even worse,
I was sent to bed without me tae and I
    had welts across me arse.

Old Biddy Ball went in one time with a
    parcel under her armpit,
"It's the same thing as usual," she said,
    "you don't even have to open it."
Arthur gave her a ten bob note, and he
    shelved it without even checking.
When he opened it up later that day, he
    did a terrible lot of fecking.

Inside that big fat bundle was stuffed,
    with tattered clothes to the brim.
Sure even half a mile away, we could
    hear the screams from within.
"Aye, there's no one as brave as a pawnbroker,"
    we could hear his raging calls,
"And we've got more than any man's got,
    for we've got three brass balls."

84

Another method of generating some income was to save up all the old worn out clothes to take to the rag store; woollens were kept separate because the store man paid a few pence a stone more for them. The rag store owned by James Morgan and Sons in the Lecky Road also bought scrap iron, copper and brass. The clothes that people took to the rag stores in those days were really rags because everything was used and handed down and reused in every household till finally into the ragbag they went.

We discovered a messy way to get some extra pocket money by following the Corporation employee with his horse and cart as he removed the mud from the street gratings. Johnny Orr was his name, from Rosemount, and he lifted the grating lids and scooped out the mud onto the gutters where it lay for a while until all the water drained away before he shovelled it onto his cart. While the mud was draining, we poked through it with our fingers to find any coins that were accidentally dropped into the grating. We always found money in the ones outside McMenamin's shop at the bottom of the banking in St Columb's Wells. At times, whenever we were getting in Johnny Orr's way, he would chase us by threatening to give us a good 'steever' (kick) on the backside.

Buried Treasure on the Banking

One afternoon, two of my pals and I were picking and eating soolick leaves that grew in small clumps on certain parts of the banking; these were small green leaves about two inches long and they tasted like very sour apples. As we were hunched over on our knees picking away, we saw two strange men coming onto the banking from the Butcher's Gate direction. We knew they hadn't seen us because we were huddling down low. They were carrying a brown Hessian bag and a trowel, and we watched them as they went over to the steep slope behind Walker's Square and pulled up a big sod of grass and dug a hole. One of the men was looking around to see if anybody was watching them as the other one put the bag into the hole, put the clay back and replaced the sod. Their secret task completed, they left the banking in the same direction as they had come.

After they left, we scurried over and removed the sod and scooped out the clay with a piece of broken slate to uncover the Hessian bag. I opened it and inside was a black metal cash box, tied shut with a piece of cord. I was feeling a bit scared and guilty as we whispered to each other and looked around to make sure there was nobody watching us. I opened the box and found a white five-pound note, two ten shilling notes and a pile of silver and copper coins. There were also some photographs, a list of names, and two sticks of red sealing wax. We quickly put everything back into the sack and reburied it. Then we put the sod back in place and promised each other not to tell anyone in case we would get into trouble.

Over the next couple of weeks, we saw the men on the banking, poking and searching for the spot where they had hidden the sack but they didn't seem to be able to find it again. My pals and I looked for it weeks later and couldn't find it either. It could still be buried there after all those years, hidden beneath the clay in the banking between Walker's Square and St Columb's Wells.

Mrs McDermott from Nailor's Row and her two children walking along the top of the banking towards Walker's Square in the 1950s. (Courtesy Mickey Gillespie.)

Banking Visitors and Hidden Banknotes

Every three or four months, four young men carried large carpets onto the banking and spread them out on the grass to beat the dust out of them with bamboo sticks and wicker beaters shaped like tennis racquets. We helped them to beat the carpets for about two hours and then they rolled them up again and carried them on their shoulders, back to God knows where as we never asked them any questions at the time. I learned later the carpets were from the mayor's parlour in the Guildhall and that one of the men was Willie Curran, a well-known local footballer who worked for Derry Corporation.

Sometimes a horse dealer, after cleaning out his stables, came with a horse and cart to the banking, and the cart was piled high with straw and horse's dung. He would dump the load over the broken-down wall at the top, just behind Friel's Terrace, and when he left, we would have great fun for a couple of hours jumping down off the wall and landing on the soft dung. It wasn't as smelly or dirty as cow or pig dung, and it was cleaner.

Nelson Street to the Lecky Road, with Derry's Walls, Walker's Pillar and the Free Masons' Hall on the skyline. At the top of the banking is Friel's Terrace and part of lower Nailor's Row in the 1940s. (Courtesy Rev B Canning.)

The only problem was that when we went home we were made to take off all our clothes and get scrubbed in the tin bath in the back yard.

One morning when I was playing on the banking behind Nailor's Row, I was poking at a loose stone in a yard wall when it fell out. Curious, I put my hand into the cavity and pulled out a bundle of banknotes tied with a piece of string. There were big white notes, red notes and green notes. I had never held a banknote before and now here I was with a bundle of them that I could just about get both my hands around. I brought the notes home to my father who took them to the Strand Road police station. I didn't know how much there was in the bundle and we never heard anything more about it after that day.

Willie the Soldier

Early one morning, my father came into the bedroom to awaken Willie for work. Willie worked with my father as an apprentice plumber for Derry Gaslight Company but on this particular day, he wasn't in his bed because he had risen before dawn and left the house. He sent a letter the following week from England to say he had joined the British army. He was eighteen years old at the time and I was proud to think that my brother was in the army. I was also glad because there was now more room for me in the bed, where Freddie and me slept at the bottom, between Paddy and Mickey and Willie's smelly feet.

St Columba

St Columba broke the winda and he blamed it on St John.
St John blamed it on St Peter and St Peter never let on.

St Columba became Derry's patron saint because he is reputed to have built a monastery in the area in the sixth century. The area was later to become known as Doire, the old Gaelic name meaning Oak Grove. St Columba's Roman Catholic Church (known as the Long Tower) outside the Walls and St Columb's Church of Ireland Cathedral, which stands inside the Walls of the old town, are dedicated to him.

The saint's feast day is celebrated on the ninth of June and when I was a boy, everybody wore an oak leaf pinned to their lapels or hats on that special day. People hung coloured buntings in the streets and religious flags from their windows, and an arch of leaves and flowers was built in St Columb's Wells. A pump beside the arch that drew water from a holy well was beautifully decorated and painted with green and gold paint. It attracted lots of people from all over the city who took holy water home with them to sprinkle in their homes and on their animals and land, praying that St Columba would protect them from all harm and evil.

People in general were tidy and most of them painted the outside walls and window frames of their houses every year in preparation for the feast day of St Columba. Unlike today, there were few slogans or murals painted on walls or the gable ends of houses. In the Fountain there was a mural painted on a gable wall of King William on a white horse, and a few slogans saying, 'God Save the Queen'. The only slogans I can remember in the nationalist areas were, 'God Save St Patrick', and one near the Brandywell innocently saying, 'God Bless Our Lord'. Those apart, there was no other graffiti on any wall and no litter on the streets.

Cleaning, Shops and Shopping

A common sight was to see women washing and scrubbing a half-moon shape on the pavement outside their front door. The brass knockers and door handles were shined with Brasso and the linoleum in the front hallway was polished, and many times an unsuspecting person when entering the house slipped on the hall mat and ended up in a heap at the bottom of the stairs. If it was the husband who came sliding in from the front door, he would threaten to spread sand on the floor, but he always saw the funny side when he got his dinner and swallowed his pride along with it.

Every Saturday, my mother sent us to get red ochre from McMichael's ships' chandlers shop in Sackville Street. She or my Aunt Julia mixed some paraffin oil and a grated candle with the ochre to

A busy sunny day in Rossville Street in the late 1950s. Note the little boys delivering the newspapers. (Courtesy E Melaugh http://cain.ulst.ac.uk/melaugh/)

make red polish which they put on the front doorstep and the living room floor. It had a lovely clean fresh smell. I remember one time when the lino was badly scuffed and needed renewing, Julia took all the furniture out of the room and turned it over. Then she applied a good coat of red polish and it lasted another couple of years.

On Saturdays, my half-sister Kathleen would send me to get her a bottle of leg tan from Young's Chemists on the Strand Road. She was about eighteen and couldn't afford silk stockings, and tights weren't about then in the early forties. She would put the tan on her legs and then draw a black line up the back of them to represent stocking seams.

Bigger's Pork Stores on Foyle Street killed pigs and cured the meat, and we were sent there once a week to buy a selection of chain bones, pig's feet, ribs and pig's hawks, and sometimes a pig's cheek or a piece of liver. The meat was very greasy but lovely and tasty when cooked along with potatoes and cabbage.

There were no fridges so the groceries were bought daily. We got most of our provisions from McHugh's shop on Bishop Street and sometimes

Cobble-stoned William Street in the 1930s. (Courtesy Margaret Brown.)

from Pat Hegarty's on Walker's Square. John McHugh's grocery shop had a barrel of salted fish outside the front door, and inside had hams and dried ling fish hanging from the ceiling. Everything was sold loose and scooped out of the storage bins to be weighed and poured into brown paper bags; items such as sugar, tea, flour, and barley, peas and lentils for making soup. All of the grocery stores were the same and the mixed smells of everything together in the shop were overpowering at times. None of these shops sold milk which had to be bought from Arthur Breslin's dairy shop in Bishop Street, where one could also buy cheeses and other dairy products.

In the warm weather, when we bought butter and margarine, we stored them in a box with a wire netting door. The wire kept the cats and rats and birds from eating the contents. The box was hung on the wall in the shadiest and coolest place in the back yard as it was the only way the butter could be kept from melting.

Further down Bishop Street from McHugh's was John Gibbon's butcher shop where my mother bought the mince for some of our daily dinners and the sausages for my father's Sunday breakfast. Beside Gibbon's was Mrs Murray's small confectionery shop that never seemed to have many sweets displayed in the window or on the shelves. Next door was Hunter's Rock Bakery Company bread shop where we purchased some of our bread. James McGirr sold fruit and vegetables beside Hunter's Bakery where we were able to get a limited amount of greens and potatoes daily. Above the shop door and windows was a sun canopy to protect and keep the vegetables that were displayed outside, cool and fresh. The shop was owned in later years by Elizabeth and William Hippsley.

"Nobody leaves this barber's shop half cut." Charley Noble's Barber's shop in Carlisle Road in the 1930s. (Courtesy Doreen Rice Wray, Central Library.)

Frances Brady's wee shop was at the top of Fahan Street, just outside Butcher's Gate at the bottom of Nailor's Row. It was triangular in shape and only about five feet long at the back wall. The counter was about four feet long and the door took up most of the front wall. Frances sold small items like salt, pepper and hair clips, and there was a net hanging down over the row of shelves on the back wall that held dozens of small packets of wares. The net was there to prevent items being accidentally knocked off the shelves whenever there was a 'crowd' of three or four customers in the premises.

There was also a clothes shop at the top of Waterloo Street, facing Butcher's Gate, which had coats and dresses hung outside on display. The shop owner's name was Doherty.

In the mornings, we went down to Sonny Fleming's Bakery on Rossville Street to get a dozen baps. Sonny made the tastiest baps in Derry and people came from all over the town to queue up to buy them; I didn't like the ones with the caraway seed in them that were known locally as 'carvy baps'. Next door to Sonny's was John McCandless's grocery shop where he recharged the wet batteries for the old wirelesses.

Also on Rossville Street, as well as the homes, shops and pubs, were the Public Baths. There were about ten large iron baths and each one was partitioned off separately. Whenever my pal Jimmy Lynch was sent there every week or so to get himself bathed and scrubbed, I went along with him. He paid a shilling to the caretaker who filled the bath with warm water then gave Jimmy a big rough towel. I paid nothing and went into the cubicle along with Jimmy. We both took off all our clothes and climbed into the lovely warm water to splash about. There was much more room in it than in the big galvanised tin bath we used at home. It was cleaner too because at home, all the youngsters were bathed in the same bath water.

It was great fun standing on the edge of the bath and jumping into the water, just the way Tarzan dived into the river to fight crocodiles to rescue his mate Jane. When we were in too long and got too noisy, the caretaker would come into the cubicle and tell us to get dried and clear off home and not to come back again. He always threatened to bar us but relented the next time we arrived.

The Plummer brothers and the Doherty baby in its pram outside its mother's shop at the top of Waterloo Street facing Butcher's Gate. In the background are the Apprentice Boys' Memorial Hall and Walker's Pillar on Derry's Walls overlooking the bottom of Nailor's Row (1940s). (Courtesy Aidan Gallagher.)

The Skull and Mayflowers

One day when I was about nine or ten, Freddie, Danny and I went out along the railway line that ran along the River Foyle and Letterkenny Road for a bit of adventure with a few pals including Cathal and Jimmy Lynch. We climbed over a gate with a notice warning trespassers that they would be prosecuted for going onto the railway lines. We weren't too aware of the danger of being hit by one of the trains that frequently passed on their way with passengers and freight to Strabane and Dublin.

We walked out along the line, gathering blackberries and throwing stones into the river, and playing in the paths that went through the trees, known as the secret passages. Whenever a train came puffing up the line, we all hid because the engineers always reported anyone seen trespassing on the line when they arrived at the next station and the police would be called.

On our way back home along the line, I was poking among some brambles near the water when I found a human skull lying above the high water line, half covered with gravel. The lower jaw was missing but it still had some of its upper teeth and three big round holes where the eyes and nose had once been. I called for a couple of my pals to come and look and as we were all examining it, somebody shouted to us that a train was coming. I threw the skull back into the brambles before running across the line and into the shelter of the trees. We continued on home and left the skull to rest in peace (or until somebody else found it.)

I often wondered who the person was; had it been a sailor who had fallen overboard and drowned far from his home? Was it someone who had accidentally fallen into the river or had committed suicide, or was it a person who had been murdered? We never told any adults about the find, or about us trespassing on the railway line, in case we would have gotten into trouble, but I have never forgotten about that gruesome find I made when I was only a young boy.

I also went during May with my brothers and sisters to the other side of the River Foyle, to a place called the Bolies, which means a summer pasture, when people were setting up altars in their homes to honour the Virgin Mary. Our older cousin Bridget Lynch took us there to gather bluebells to place on our own May altar at home. Other children were doing likewise and on the long walk home we found lots of dropped bluebells scattered along the way.

It was nice to see the flowers in the two glass vases on each side of Our Lady's statue. It was the only time we saw them in the house because they weren't too plentiful in the town then. The only other places you could see flowers were on the front of the altar in the Long Tower Church or the pond in Brooke Park when we were taken with my mother to see the fish. The pond had a low netting wire fence around it and the fish swam under the lily pads, with the white lilies growing out of the water.

Religion, First Communion and the Loose Tooth

Rev Willie Doherty who was the main force behind the construction of the Long Tower Church which he dedicated to Saint Columba, the patron saint of Derry. (Courtesy Rev B Canning.)

St Columba's Church was our parish and every Sunday morning, all the school children went to ten o'clock Mass. Freddie, Danny and I went to the Christian Brothers Brow of the Hill School, as had our uncles, so we sat in the left-hand gallery. Other sections of the church were allocated to the Bridge Street, Long Tower Boys, Convent of Mercy, and the 'Wee Nuns' schools. Every teacher looked after their own section, and if a pupil didn't turn up at Mass, the teacher or Christian Brother would be very cross on Monday morning and ask them why they hadn't been to church on Sunday. If you hadn't a good excuse, or went to another Mass or church, you were punished and got six slaps on the hands with a stick or a thick leather strap.

A religious procession passing the Gasworks yard on the Lecky Road in 1945.
(Courtesy Eddie Moore.)

The pupils went to confessions every month and devotions every evening in October, and nobody ever spoke or made a noise in the church during the ceremony. It was lovely and peaceful whenever we were all singing the hymns, *Tantum Ergo* and *Adoramus,* and smelling the incense which reminded me of burnt sandalwood as it rose from the altar to the ceiling, and seeing all the candles burning in front of the exposed Blessed Eucharist on the altar.

My mother and Julia loved the Long Tower Church and went every day to pray. It was there I made my First Confession and First Communion when I was six years old. I remember my First Confession, kneeling in the darkness until the priest slid the little hatch door open. I told him all my sins, about stealing the sugar and putting my tongue out at my Aunt Julia, and pulling my sister's hair and saying bad words. I was given one Our Father and a Hail Mary to say for my penance, and

School-children coming home along the top of the banking behind Walker's Square from the 'Wee Nuns' school, Long Tower, 1950s. (Courtesy Patricia Deery.)

I knew that my Guardian Angel walked beside me with a big smile on its face on my way home.

On the day of my First Communion, I was scrubbed clean and dressed in my new black suit with a big Sacred Heart badge pinned on the lapel. My mother also put a new string on my Miraculous Medal and hung it around my neck, and as I walked to the church with my hands joined together under my chin, I felt so holy. When I was kneeling in the church among the hundreds of other boys and girls, my stomach was rumbling with hunger because we had to fast from the previous night before receiving the Holy Communion.

Then a terrible disaster happened to me: I swallowed a loose tooth, right down into my empty stomach where my first ever Holy Communion was going to be in another couple of minutes. In my childish innocence, I believed that nothing else was supposed to be in there, along with God, and now he was going to be joined by a tooth. I was very fearful as I put out my tongue to receive the Blessed Sacrament and tried to remember all the things I had been told to do – and not to do – on this very holy occasion, such as not to let the Host touch your teeth but to swallow it as quickly as possible. But I was also supposed to have an empty stomach so I believed I was committing a grave sin on my First Communion day and I couldn't do anything about it because of the tooth. I even wondered if my Guardian Angel had deserted me or not. I closed my eyes and expected the worst, and was overjoyed when my tongue didn't shrivel up when He was placed on it, and there was no commotion from God in my stomach when He landed on my tooth.

I told the priest about the sin at my next confession and he told me to say a Hail Mary for my penance. I was taken to visit all my aunts and uncles that First Communion day and was richer both in spirit and pocket at the end of the day, especially pocket, as I had collected six shillings.

Arch erected across Rossville Street during the Eucharistic Congress of 1932. (Courtesy David Bigger collection.)

Death of Wee Hughie

One Sunday morning after Mass in 1945, I was sitting at the table by the window reading the Beano comic. It was peaceful and quiet, and my mother was preparing the dinner on the top of the fire range. Everyone else except my father, who always went to twelve o'clock Mass, was out at church, and the younger ones were outside playing. My father came in from the front room where he and my mother slept with my youngest brother Hughie, a Down's syndrome baby, who was only four years old. He was holding his hand to his chest and throat, and was very upset. He said to my mother, "Wee Hughie is dead," and I felt a terrifying panic as I jumped up from my chair and ran out into the street, not knowing what to do.

I ran around to the banking where Freddie was playing near Walker's Square and with a great lump and tightness in my throat, I repeated to him what my father had said to my mother, "Wee Hughie is dead." We both ran back to the house with the tears streaming down our cheeks.

We were shattered. Hughie was our youngest brother and he had always waited for us with a big smile to come in from school every day as he sat up in his pram. He had never walked but was a great joy to us all with his pleasant smile and the big wave combed into his blond hair. Now he was gone, leaving a great longing in me to have just one more glimpse of his smiling blue eyes.

When he was laid out in a white baby coffin, I stood looking at him for a long time as I touched his little cold hands hoping he would open his eyes and smile at me. All of our relations, friends and neighbours followed his coffin, carried to the city cemetery by my father and the older males of our household. There seemed to be hundreds at Wee Hughie's funeral, and the words I had read in my mother's prayer book came to mind, "And a little child shall lead them."

That night after the funeral, when we were lying in our beds in the darkness, we sobbed our eyes out until sleep came upon us to soothe and rest our heavy hearts.

Passing Lives
(To Hughie)
by Phil Cunningham

In this sunlit place by my window I sit, wrapped in a gown of quiet
contented peace.
Only the ticking of the clock on the mantelpiece shelf to regulate
And record the life that is and passing on.
Mother softly singing whilst she tidies the room to a new day.
In the other room, a bedroom where a Down's syndrome child sleeps,
The curtains silently close to end his part, an Angel in life's drama.
No drums or trumpets to sound a farewell.
Only the ticking of a mantelpiece clock heralds the passing and birth
of a new Angel.

Father Monagle – Priest,
Entrepreneur and Daredevil

The Long Tower parish Church was the heart and hub of the whole area from the Brandywell to the top of Fahan Street. All fund raising activities, such as parades, sports and concerts that were organised by the people, were encouraged and promoted by Father Monagle, the parish priest. He was respected and feared by both young and old alike.

The men and boys raised their caps or saluted him whenever he passed by and the women and girls nodded their heads to him. He would come into our house sometimes in the cold weather and stand with his back to the fire with his coat tails lifted up warming his rear end. If my mother happened to be sewing, knitting or baking scones, he would ask her if they were for his sale of work that he held regularly to raise money for the church building fund. The Catholic Church had to build and maintain its own schools and churches without state benefits in those days. Patrick Cleary was the sacristan of the church until Willie McCay from Friel's Terrace replaced him for many years after.

Father Monagle had an old Ford car when he first came to the Long Tower parish. One memorable day, he drove the car down Nailor's Row

Marching majorettes lead the Long Tower Carnival parade past Coulhoun's Bakery and the Arch Bar on its way through Bishop's Gate in the 1950s. (Courtesy Patricia McAdams, Central Library.)

and down Primrose Lane in the banking to the bottom of Fahan Street, and on down through Fox's Corner to Rossville Street and the Lecky Road. He was the talk of the whole parish for doing what was regarded as a daredevil act, driving a car down such a precarious path.

On another memorable occasion, a card school was in progress near the gate at the end of Walker's Square with a pile of coins on the ground in the centre of the excited card players. Like a bolt from the blue, Father Monagle suddenly rushed through the gateway from Nailor's Row towards the gamblers who scattered, leaving all the bets and cards

The Derry City Building Fund carnival coming down Linenhall Street from Ferryquay Street in 1954.
(Courtesy Charley Logue.)

behind them. Father Monagle collected all the money and walked over to the other end of the Square where he was suddenly confronted by one of the gamblers, a small stocky man with leggings up to his knees and a brimmed hat. The man cursed at Father Monagle and called him a few unsavoury names, and the priest took out his crucifix and held it up between him and the man as he walked backwards out of the Square.

Another day, Freddie and I were playing on the banking on a school holiday for us in the Christian Brothers although all the other schools were open. We were the only two boys on the banking that day and when we heard a shout, we looked around to see Father Monagle beckoning us over. We were a bit frightened when he asked us why we were not at school and he didn't believe us when we told him we were off on a holiday so he took us up to our mother to see if we were telling lies. When she confirmed we were off school for the day, he told us to run away out and enjoy ourselves; we were so relieved to be released from his attention.

There was a wake in one of the houses one day and, as was the custom, Father Monagle heard confessions the night before the funeral in one of the bedrooms in the wake house. Due to a shortage of space, everyone had to make their confession to him as he sat behind the bedroom door. There was an old spinster who lodged in the house who spent much of her time praying in the Long Tower Church. When it was her turn for confession, she entered the room blessing herself and whispering prayers. Then she opened the wardrobe door, which was facing her, went inside, closed the door behind her and knelt down. On realising she had mistaken the wardrobe for a confessional box, she quickly hurried out again to find Father Monagle sitting grinning at her from behind the door trying to hold in his laughter. In her embarrassment, she stormed out of the room, slamming the door behind her, and rushed down the stairs to the street. This hasty exit made everyone wonder just what she had confessed to be given a penance that put her in such a great fluster.

The Blacksmith's Forge

At the end of Maeve's Row on the Lecky Road, facing the Bluebell Bar, was Alex and George Hassan's forge. It was built against the retaining wall of Hogg's Folly and was a whitewashed quarry stone structure with a black-tarred felt roof. My school friends and I, on our way home from school, sometimes stopped to look at the smithy working the bellows to redden the fire from which he took a white-hot piece of iron to place on the large anvil. The red and white sparks shot skywards as he shaped it with his hammer into a horseshoe, which he dipped into a trough of cold water where it hissed and sent up a cloud of steam. Then he lifted the horse's leg and, with his back to the animal, held its hoof between his knees to pare it down with a sharp knife before giving it a good rub with a rasp file.

The iron shoe was re-heated before Alex placed it on the hoof, causing it to singe, and the smoke from it smelt like burning hair. He held about a dozen flat iron nails between his teeth as he nailed the shoe onto the horse's hoof. Seeing him hammer them in made us all cringe, believing that the poor horse was in pain, but we were told that it didn't feel anything. After Alex was finished shoeing it, he led it outside where its owner then yoked it back into its cart. Before the next horse was led into the forge to be shod, we were chased away from the smithy door and told to run away home to do our homeworks.

In those days, the bread, milk and carrier companies, such as Deery's Old City Milk Dairy and Wordie's Transport, used horse-drawn vehicles and employed smiths in their own farrieries to tend to the horses.

Schools and Concerts

The first two years of my schooling were in the Sisters of Mercy Convent School on Artillery Street where I was given a slate to learn to write on with white chalk, and not very successfully taught to use knitting needles. My sisters and cousin Bridget Lynch went there too. Bridget took us to school and back, and woe betide anyone who tried to be nasty with us because Bridget would give them a clout. We felt very safe and secure when she was along with us.

It was a much different world when I was sent to the Christian Brothers on the Brow of the Hill where I was often stopped by two or three boys coming down Hogg's Folly from their school, the Long Tower Boys. They would hold me up against the wall and take every thing out of my schoolbag, and sometimes would punch me in the stomach. Eventually, my older stepbrothers found out what was happening and suddenly the bullying stopped.

I got on very well at the Christian Brothers and was selected to sing in the school concerts and choirs which won many competitions at the Derry Feis over the years. The only thing I didn't like about being in the choir was having to stay in school after lessons to practise when everyone else had gone home. This also meant I was late doing my homework when the rest of my pals were playing on the banking. I liked being in the concerts when they were in St Columb's Hall all week because we got tea and buns back stage when the concert was over, and I was allowed to go to school an hour later than the rest of the boys each morning.

I remember one scene in a concert when I was dressed as a girl in a beautiful green ballroom dress that took my mother a week to make. There were dozens of sequins sewn onto it and it looked beautiful as they sparkled like jewels under the lights. I also had to wear a mantilla as a headpiece and Joe Quigley was my partner in the ballroom dance. If the spectators had only known that underneath that lovely dress I was feeling a bit draughty because in those days most boys didn't wear any underpants and I was one of them. So, if a sudden breeze had blown onto the stage and lifted my dress, the moon would have been shining as well as the sequins.

My cousin John McGinley sang a song called *You're a Little Too Small* in the cowboy scene and Hugh 'Whitey' O'Neill sang the popular song of the time, *Love Thee Dearest, Love Thee*. At the end of the concert every night, the choir sang the rousing marching song *A Nation Once Again* to a standing ovation from the audience. Some of the braver boys would sing: "Starvation once again, starvation once again. No bread, no butter, no sugar, no tea, starvation once again."

The Confirmation class of the Christian Brothers Brow of the Hill School in 1945. Back row, from left: Unknown, S McAnee, Unknown, N McKeown, N Gorman, Unknown, J Bradley, D Walsh, R O'Connell, Unknown, C McDermott, Unknown, Unknown, J McKinley and J McMenamin. Fourth row, from left: Unknown, B McFadden, Unknown, R McDaid, Unknown, T Doherty, J McLaughlin, J Lyttle, Wally Ferry, B Burke, J McGinley, M Mallett, D Boyle and Unknown. Third row, from left: H Doherty, Unknown, J McCloskey, T McIntyre, M Roddy, G McDonagh, J B McLaughlin, J Bonnar, J Sullivan, B McDermott, Unknown and T McGlinchey. Second row, from left: Unknown, E McKeever, D McConnologue, J Cullion, B Boyle, D Toland, R McDermott, B Arthur, C Morrison, H Sheerin, J Gallagher and P Morrison. Front row, from left: Joe Kelly, Jude O'Brien, J Nelis, W McCorriston, F Campbell, L Jackson, J Friel, L Kitson, N Crumlish and T Cassidy. (Courtesy John McGinley.)

108

Participants in the cowboy scene in the Christian Brothers' "Our Boys" concert held in St Columb's Hall in the 1940s. The star of the scene was John McGinley; seen standing at the back, who sang *You're a Little Too Small*. Back row, from left: R McQuaid, J Burns, R Coyle, J McGinley, B Coyle, L Murphy and D Reddin. Middle row, from left: R Brown, G Hegarry, D Casey, B Doherty, S Cowley, J McIntyre and Junior McDaid. Kneeling, from left: J Lamberton, N Reddin, B Boyle, G Kilkie, H Coyle and Seamus McAnee. (Courtesy John McGinley.)

109

Brother McFarland, Tommy Carr and Paddy Carlin taught us the songs and the acting scenes. Tommy and Paddy were friendly teachers, especially Paddy who always had a big smile on his face whenever he spoke to you. Brother 'Spanky' McFarland was strict and whenever he heard someone singing flat notes or out of tune, he went round everyone until he found the culprit. Then he put the stick that he used for slapping into the boy's mouth and rattled it up and down against his teeth to make him keep his mouth wide open when he was singing. No losers were acceptable in his book whenever the choir sang in the Derry Feis and discipline was the order of the day. We must win in the Gregorian chant or be damned!

Another teacher I felt at ease with because of his courteous calm nature was Brian Friel. Whenever he taught us English he gave us books to read and the classroom went quiet for an hour as everyone enjoyed the popular stories of the time such as *The Last of the Mohicans, Beau Geste* and *Gulliver's Travels*. Brian went on to become a very successful author and playwright with *Philadelphia, Here I Come* and many others including, *Dancing at Lughnasa* which was made into a film.

Homeboys

There were quite a few abandoned and orphaned children at the Christian Brothers School and they were called Homeboys because they were housed in the orphan's home on Termonbacca Hill. It seemed to me that the Christian Brothers treated them harsher than the rest of us and some boys felt pity for them because of this. On the other hand, I noticed the Homeboys were always well clothed and always had on good stout boots and warm socks, and on rainy days, they wore good raincoats. I also knew that they always had a warm breakfast of porridge, tea and bread before they came out to school each morning. In fact, many of us with loving parents had less comfortable clothes to wear, and only had a crust to eat (if we were lucky) before we came to school in the mornings. Still, I would not have changed places with any one of them.

Ailments and Cures

Paddy McGinty

Paddy McGinty had a rubber doll.
He washed it and dried it and then he let it fall.
He sent for the doctor, the doctor couldn't come,
Because he had a pimple on his wee bare bum.

When I was about ten years old, my half brother Willie, who had run away to join the army, came home on leave to get married to Eileen Quigley from Howard's Street. The wedding reception was held in her parents' house where we went to be given lemonade and biscuits, and my mother and father and Julia got their tea. A week later, Willie was gone again for another few years. He was stationed in Hong Kong and won a few medals, not for beating the enemy but for defeating his opponents when he fought for the army boxing team. Paddy got married too and my cousin Willie Cooley married Mary Donnelly from Sloan's Terrace, so that was four gone from the house in a few short

Author's stepbrothers Mickey and Paddy clowning about in the back yard in 1949.

years, including wee Hughie who died earlier. That now left just fourteen of us living in the one house.

My Uncle Freddie Cooley was a small man of slight build who worked in Bannigan's fruit store on Foyle Street for a few years before working in Doherty's scrap iron yard on the same street for ten years. He was a good-tempered man who never went to his bed without first kneeling beside it to say his prayers. Whenever he came home on a Friday with his meagre wages, he gave them to my mother and told her to see to the weans first, and then, if there was anything left, she would give him enough to bet on a few horses and buy some cigarettes. He loved reading cowboy books and early each evening in the winter, he went to bed to read by candlelight. He had a hobby making wooden toys on a fretwork pedal machine in the bedroom which he painted and gave to us. Freddie died in our house in Creggan with lung cancer at the age of forty-seven and I helped my father lift him out of bed to wash his body for burial.

Paddy came back to the house a year after his marriage. His wife Molly (née McColgan) had died along with their unborn child.

The whole of Ireland was rife with tuberculosis during those years so it was not surprising that our family would suffer also when my elder brother Mickey was taken into St Columb's chest hospital with the ailment. I remember the X-ray vans coming round the streets to examine everyone and hundreds of people were taken into hospital, where dozens died with the disease in Derry alone. People were afraid to speak about TB, it was so widespread, and if anyone mentioned the dreaded word, it was said in a whisper, or called consumption, in case they would contract it themselves.

We were taken to the hospital to see Mickey every week for about two years while he was recovering from having a lung removed. Everybody in the house had to be X-rayed and I was found to have a defect in my lung and was put into the Royal Victoria Hospital in Belfast for a month to be operated on.

Other afflictions that were common then, were scabies, squints, rickets, carbuncles, gumboils, ulcers of the stomach, diarrhoea, bunions, asthma, sore eyes, scally eyes and hen toes, to name but a few.

Bugs, fleas and head lice were some of the other annoyances that families had to put up with. There was a concerted effort by the health authorities to try to eradicate the pests from the schools and homes and it wasn't uncommon to see children with their heads shaved. The health inspector was called Nurse Pitts and the children used to chant: "Nurse Pitts, has fits, whenever she sees nits."

Some home made remedies for the common afflictions and ailments were: Sloan's liniment, baking soda, poultices, beetroot in stout for tonics, brown paper over the chest to brave the cold, drops of peroxide into the ear to ease ear ache, and whiskey or poteen for most other ailments.

Anyone who had chapped hands from working outdoors in the cold weather rubbed oatmeal into the affected areas. A wart on the skin was rubbed with half a potato with a cross cut into it that was then thrown away outside. Itchy spots and rashes were treated with spittle first thing in the morning before eating.

To bolster immunity to colds, flus and stomach ailments in the winter, Julia or my mother made a pot of porridge at bedtimes that had to boil for about half an hour. We called it brochan and it tasted thick and gooey, and we added sugar and milk to it if we had any in the house. Most adults put salt on theirs at night and sugar in the morning.

A loose tooth was extracted by tying a string to it and the other end to a boot or shoe before it was dropped over the banister at the top of the stairs. Alternatively, one could tie the string to a door handle and sit waiting on a chair until somebody came along and opened the door, thus pulling out the loose tooth. You had to make sure you didn't tie the string to the wrong side of the door and have some other teeth knocked out or get a black eye when it was opened

I remember the day I tried this DIY extraction method and when I threw the boot over the banister rail at the top of the stairs, nothing happened. The tooth refused to budge and the boot was dangling in mid air with me moaning in agony as I tried to grab the string in order to take the weight off it. I had to wait another couple of days to do it all over again when the tooth had loosened more.

In the summer, we were allowed to play outside without wearing any shoes. Sometimes one of us would get a stony bruise which was caused when a small sharp stone embedded itself into the sole of the foot and the skin grew back over it again, causing it to fester. It was a painful bruise and the foot had to be bathed in warm water to soften the skin so the stone could be poked out with a sewing needle or a pin that had been sterilised over a flame.

A painful nettle sting was cured by rubbing the affected area with a freshly plucked docking leaf and repeating the words, "Docking in, nettle out." Most times the cure worked.

Scarlet fever was a common illness, and Freddie caught it when he was three years old. He was put into the fever hospital on Foyle Hill and I remember health officials sealing up the bedroom door after they had lighted a sulphur candle inside the room to fumigate it.

If someone dropped a piece of food onto the ground, they lifted it and kissed it, then offered it up to God before eating it. That was done to remove anything evil or harmful that might have contaminated it when it was lying there.

Whenever anybody had a hole in the sole of their shoe, they cut out a piece of cardboard or lino and inserted it into the shoe to keep the rain out. This was only a temporary repair, especially on a very wet day. If a boy was courting a girl and he had a hole in the heel of his sock that showed above the back of his shoe, he blackened his bare heel with shoe polish so that the white skin would be less noticeable through the hole.

Summer Holidays

In the summer, Julia and my mother spent a week washing all the bedclothes in the back yard. They filled a big tin bath with warm water and rubbed the bedclothes with a bar of soap. Then they scrubbed them up and down on the washboard which was a wooden frame with a sheet of ribbed galvanised tin in it that stood in the bath of water. The clothes were then wrung out by hand and hung up to dry on the washing-lines.

On a sunny summer's day, usually a Sunday, we all went to the Daisyfield on the Letterkenny Road to have a picnic. My younger sisters, Mary and Helen, were pushed in their prams and us boys and

Susie and Margaret, walked or ran excitedly in front. We had sandwiches wrapped in brown paper, bottles of diluted orange juice and sugared water, and sometimes a packet of plain biscuits, all packed into the bottom of the prams. Many families did the same thing and the field was filled with children playing while the mothers sat chatting on the grass. The men sat on the low wall near the road, smoking their pipes and talking and laughing as well as keeping an eye on the road for the odd car or horse and trap to pass by to wave to the drivers. Other men passed by with their girlfriends or walking their greyhounds.

Whenever the train was heard puffing its way out of the railway station from the Foyle Road, or in from the Lifford direction, we all ran to the gate or the fence to watch and wave to the driver and his passengers who waved back to us. After the long evening playing, running, jumping and chasing, everything was gathered up and we wearily made our way home. Over Anne Street, through the Brandywell and up Hogg's Folly, then up Long Tower Street and down the brae to Nailor's Row, and finally into number two Friel's Terrace. The bed was lovely and cosy, and sleep came as soon as my head rested on my pillow.

Fanad Peninsula

Where do you come from?
Donegal.
How's your praties?
Big and small.
How do you eat them?
Skins and all.
Do they not choke you?
Not at all.

During the summer holidays, my father took Freddie, Danny and I to visit our mother's relations who lived about four miles past Rathmullan on the Fanad peninsula in County Donegal. We went on the Lough Swilly train to Fahan and got a small ferryboat near the big pier across the Lough to Rathmullan. We then had to walk the four miles to the

The dishes are all washed and the spuds are on in Thomas Street in 1945. From left: Eddie Moore, Granny McCool, Lily Casey (Jnr), Granny Moore, Lily McElhinney and Lily Casey (Snr). (Courtesy Eddie Moore.)

hill of Laharden (the gentle or small hill), near the Knockalla Mountain where our friends, the McLaughlin, McAteer and Lynch families, lived in thatched cottages. There was no other transport, apart from a donkey that was used to carry turf from the bog in wicker creels, hand made from willow sticks or wands.

We stayed there for two weeks and it was a great novelty climbing up a ladder to the loft every night at bedtime to sleep on the straw-filled mattress and the pillows filled with chaff. Everything was cooked on a big open turf fire where the black iron pots and skillets hung from a crook that could be swung out above the smouldering hearth. Each morning, the slab stone floor was sprinkled with clean shore sand and at bedtime it was swept out with a besom into the front yard where the hens would peck and scratch through it at sunrise in search of any tasty morsels that may have fallen into it.

The 200-year-old St Mary's Church of Oughterlin was about three miles away in Glencar, behind Laharden Hill where we went to hear Sunday Mass spoken in Gaelic. The old Irish customs prevailed there where the males all sat in the left-hand side of the church and the females occupied the other side. Outside after Mass, everybody stood about for a while exchanging news and stories about their own particular areas.

The men of the locality made their livelihoods by sea fishing and whenever they came home in the evenings, they would often put two or three large crabs into the fire among the burning turf to cook. We loved to eat them along with potatoes and onions. Afterwards, we each got a slice of scone bread with butter and jam spread thickly over it, and a drink of smooth buttermilk to wash everything down.

Some days after a high tide, a couple of the young girls were sent to the shore with a white enamel bucket to collect some edible seaweed called dulse from the rocks and to gather the sand eels that were stranded after being chased ashore by larger fish. These were then boiled and eaten along with potatoes for dinner.

From the front door we could look across Lough Swilly and see the little steam train puffing round the bend at Fahan, carrying its passengers and goods to Buncrana, Clonmany and Carndonagh.

Another ferryboat that my father took us on a few times crossed the River Foyle, a couple of hundred yards downstream from Craigavon Bridge. In earlier times, traders in the Waterside used the ferry to cross the river because it was cheaper than paying the tolls charged for using the bridge. We climbed down a ladder from the wharf to get onto the boat that held about ten people, and were rowed across to the dock at Browning Drive. It was a short journey across by boat but the walk back took a lot longer.

Fires and Gypsies

Aunt Julia slept in the small upstairs back room along with Bridget, Kathleen, Susie, Margaret and Mary. There wasn't enough room for two beds so a mattress was laid down on the floor every night, and at bedtime, someone went up with a piece of lighted newspaper to ignite the gas lamp for the younger girls to get into bed. When the girls went up one night, they discovered the room was full of smoke and started screaming. My father and some of the older boys rushed up to find the mattress on the floor on fire. They had to run down to the yard and get buckets of water to throw onto the burning mattress to extinguish the fire. A piece of the burning paper that had been used to light the lamp must have fallen and set fire to the mattress. The girls all had to share the one bed that night in the smoke-stained room.

On another occasion, there was an accidental fire in the living room when Willie and my father came in to get a cup of tea on their lunch break. While my father was making the tea, Willie stood with his back to the fire, warming his buttocks. He was wearing a long raincoat and as I watched dumbfounded, the smoke rose up from behind him and then suddenly the back of his coat burst into flames. He panicked and ran into the yard, with my father running after him. I looked out of the window at them and heard my father cursing and swearing as he pulled the flaming coat off Willie and threw it down the yard. My mother ran in from the front door when she heard the commotion, and I told her that, "Me Da and Willie is fighting in the back yard." I realised later that they weren't fighting and that Willie could have been seriously injured and the house could have caught fire.

Every month or so, two female gypsies with babies in their arms came round the houses to ask for spare pennies. My mother brought them into the house and sat them on the sofa to give them a cup of tea and a slice of buttered bread. She also fed the babies. After half an hour, they would leave again, calling, "God and Mary's blessings on everybody in this house."

One day, Bob Moore's wife baked two scones and put them outside to cool on the windowsill, and after she had given the gypsies their tea, one of them put one of the scones under her shawl as she passed the window. When Mrs Moore discovered the scone missing, she called down, "God's curses on the thieving gypsies." But she soon forgave them because that was the way of life then.

Mucca Singh – Travelling Salesman

Nice clothes weren't often seen in the area in the 1940s, and they weren't easy to buy because money was scarce. One day, an Indian man carrying a large suitcase called at our door and asked if he could come in. My mother brought him in and when he opened the suitcase, all eyes stared in amazement for it contained the most colourful and beautiful blouses, scarves, dresses and ties that they had ever seen. He let them have whatever they wanted there and then, and only charged them a few shillings per week until they were paid off. This instalment method was the only way people could get nice new clothes because they couldn't afford to buy them outright in one payment from the shops.

The Indian salesman was Mucca Singh and he came to our house for many years after, until others came to the town and opened shops that offered the same repayment deals. He was the first real live coloured man we had ever seen until the American sailors came to Derry, near the end of the war. I had only ever seen one before in the movies and the school geography books.

I had often seen the dockers look like coloured men, among them my Uncle Jimmy 'Tats' Lynch and his two sons Alex and Willie, coming home from the quay after unloading the coal boats. They carried big coal shovels over their shoulders and their faces and hands were black with the coal dust that stuck to their sweat when they shovelling the coal into the huge buckets that were lowered into the boat by crane. Their white eyes would look out of their black masks at us and they wore sweat scarves around their necks and string tightly tied around each leg below their knees. The scarf was to help keep the coal dust out and the string to keep the rats from running up their trouser legs when they were working in the holds of the boats.

A Horse and Cow Clap

Charlie Doherty went with a girl called Kathleen Johnston who lived next door to the Henry family in Nailor's Row. Charlie drove a horse and flat cart for Wordie's carriers on Foyle Street. When he visited Kathleen, he stopped the horse outside her door and tied its nosebag of corn under its mouth to feed. We would all climb onto the cart and wait for Charlie to come out again. When he eventually emerged, he would let us ride on the cart. It was a great experience to sit holding the reins and see the horse's big tail and hindquarters, and listen to the clip clop of its iron shoes on the road as it plodded along. Sometimes its tail went up, and big balls of brown dung dropped onto the road; it wasn't an unpleasant smell and people came out and collected it to put on their flowerpots.

The cattle market was held once a week and one of the entrances was on Joseph Street, off Fahan Street. When the cows were brought to the market, they were herded through the streets and often some of them broke away from the herders, known locally as cow wallopers, and ran to the grass on the banking, which was their natural grazing instinct. The herders chased after them and one or two of the cows ran into our street.

We were inside eating our dinners when we heard awful clattering and rumbling noises in the front hallway. One of the cows, in a panic to escape the cow wallopers, had run into our house. It was slipping and sliding on the polished oilcloth and the herders were pulling it out by the tail. My father had to beat it on the head with the sweeping

The half moon front street wash was a twice-weekly chore for many females before the mop became available in Derry.

brush to keep it from charging right into the living room and wrecking the place. After it was gone, the whole hallway had to be washed and sprinkled with disinfectant to get rid of the smell of the cow's dung that had been splattered all over the floor. That was a regular occurrence in the area.

Home Industry and Busking

The tinkers were people who made vessels and small implements from tin, hence the name 'tinker'. They came around the houses about every six months selling tin mugs, cans and jugs. They also sold long wire toasting forks, used for sticking into a slice of bread so it could be held in front of the open fire to make toast. When drinking hot tea out of the tin mug you had to be very careful or it would scald your lips. We used the tin can for carrying milk when we were sent to Harkin's house

121

at the bottom of the banking lane on St Columb's Wells. The Harkins had cows somewhere out in the country and sold the milk from their house. On my way back to the house, I often drank some of the milk and told my mother that it jibbled out as I was coming up the banking. I don't think she believed me because she went to Harkin's for milk when she was a little girl and probably did the same thing herself.

People had to earn a living and because there were few good jobs about, many came up with very inventive ways to make a few shillings such as Dan Carlin from Fahan Street who made and sold toy soldiers, Indians and cowboys with lead for a penny each, and the man who made holy medals.

John McCarron in Fahan Street sold white chalk clay pipes that were very brittle. They were easily broken so it was common to see someone smoking a pipe with only half a stem. We were often sent down to buy them for families that were holding a wake for a dead relative. The pipes and tobacco were handed out to anyone who smoked and the stems had to be rubbed with soap or wet with a spittle before they were smoked or else the pipe stem would stick to the smoker's lip and pull off a bit of skin. It was mostly women who smoked the clay pipes because men had their own wooden ones. We used to blow soap bubbles with them and that was how we found out about them pulling the skin off the lips when the pipes were dry.

There was a little man we called 'Slabbery' Mickey McLaughlin who collected jam jars. He pushed a handcart into which he put the jars he exchanged for small cardboard windmills shaped like swastikas that he made himself. We ran up and down the street with them but even against the strongest breeze, they never really revolved and soon fell apart.

Jack Pepper was a street-singer who often visited our area. He wore a shabby raincoat, tied around the middle with a piece of sisal cord, and he always sang the hymn *Faith of Our Fathers* and then collected a few pennies in his cap. Sometimes we followed him and he went into the Fountain Street and sang *God Save the Queen*. Nobody had any ill feelings towards him because everybody had their own methods to stave off the hunger and pay for their keep.

There were a lot of chimney sweeps about in those days. Three sweeps lived in Fahan Street: John Kelly, John McDaid and Frank

Seamus Smith (in middle) brightens up this 1950s scene of unemployed men in the dismal waiting room of the Labour Exchange in Bishop Street.

A meeting of the Unemployed Association in the TGWU room Orchard Street (1950s). In the middle, abstaining in the vote, is Tommy Carlin. Others include: Joe 'Morney' Stewart at the front, Tommy Green, Willie Green, Willie Stewart, Phonsie Bradley, George Campbell and Connie Glackin.

Fahan Street and the smoky Bogside below in the 1950s. Molly (Gibson) McLaughlin's Fahan Bar is on the right at the top of the street. (Courtesy Patricia Deery.)

The junction of
Fahan Street, St
Columb's Wells and
Fox's Corner in the
1950s where
Primrose Lane
emerged at the
bottom of the
banking beside
Harkin's and
Curran's houses.
(Courtesy Willie
Breslin.)

125

The Battle of Fox's Corner
Revived by Phil Cunningham

There was a battle as big as a fight,
It lasted all day and it went on all night.
They were allowed to kick and to fight,
At the battle of Fox's Corner.

Chorus
Holy Moses what a crew,
Some of them black and some of them blue,
Over the banking they all flew,
At the battle of Fox's Corner.

Over the banking they all ran,
Some of them black and some of them tan.
Biddy Coyle was choking a man,
At the battle of Fox's Corner.

Chorus

Paddy Ball hit Mickey Strong,
Over the head with a treacle scone.
They were hairing each other all day long,
At the battle of Fox's Corner.

Chorus

Barney Doherty he was there,
And was split on the head with the leg of a chair.
Dan the Ram he went on the tear,
At the battle of Fox's Corner.

Chorus

When the battle was over and everything done,
They all shook hands with everyone.
And all agreed they had great fun,
At the battle of Fox's Corner.

Chorus

Maguire who was an ex-serviceman. Another named George Hasson lived in Howard Street and Simon 'Simey' Sweeney lived in a room in the first of the old red brick houses beyond the garden gate on upper Nailor's Row. It was a double house where the McClintock and the Ferguson families lived in the biggest part of it.

There being no government benefits in those days, most of the people shared what they had and that was why some men used whatever little talents they had to make ends meet.

Eddie McDermott stayed in Annie Barr's lodging house and had a handcart which he used to carry passengers' luggage to and from the railway station for a living.

Johnny Anderson collected all sorts of bottles and returned them to the shops to claim the refund of a penny per bottle.

A short sturdy man came around the streets every three months to sharpen knives and scissors. He had a sharpening stone that was mounted on wheels, and which he operated with a foot pedal.

On Friday mornings, Francie Brandon sold fish from his handcart calling, "Fresh herring, their eyes all open, pipes in their mouths and them all smoking."

Sometimes a man stood in the middle of the street, playing an accordion, and another man played a tin whistle.

There was no public expenditure during the war years; no houses or roads were being built. The very iron ornamental railings around big houses and public buildings were being taken away and shipped to England to be melted down to make material and weapons for the war. Everything was in decay, and the bricks and houses were crumbling around the people.

War Memories – Barrage Balloons and Air Raid Shelters

When the Second World War began in 1939, the defence forces installed an anti-aircraft system around the city to protect the Derry docks which were to become a major North Atlantic naval base. A ring of huge helium-filled barrage balloons were anchored with steel cables and they floated about a hundred feet above the ground to keep enemy bomber planes from flying low over the area. We could see two of the silvery-grey-coloured balloons over Brooke Park and Pennyburn from the top of the banking. In the Diamond, two huge open-topped steel water tanks were erected for fire fighting, each about twenty feet in diameter and five or six feet high. One was outside Austin's and the other in the opposite corner of the Diamond, facing Sullivan's auctioneers. There was a young lad accidentally drowned in one of them during the war.

Air raid shelters were built in most of the streets in Derry. They were long red brick structures with no windows and concrete roofs about eight inches thick and they had slatted doors with bolts and locks. We used to climb onto them to play, until our parents would shout at us to get down. The shelters were very smelly and some nights when the air raid sirens went off, people would hide under their beds or their stairs until the all-clear siren sounded instead of going to the unpleasant shelters.

Once, an older boy said he was going to parachute off the top of the air raid shelter near our house so he took his father's bicycle and, with our help, put it on top of the shelter. Then he climbed up onto the roof with his mother's umbrella and tied it to his back. He mounted the bike and peddled as hard as he could along the roof, the idea being that when he went off the edge he would float with the aid of the umbrella to the ground. We all stood below in anticipation as he sped along the roof and plummeted over the edge, hitting the ground with the umbrella inside out and the bicycle's wheels buckling underneath him. He escaped unhurt from his experiment but I wondered if his parents let him off as lightly after damaging their belongings without their consent.

My pal Jimmy Lynch and I found some bullets on the banking one day. We lit a fire inside the air raid shelter and then threw them into it. Our parents nearly went berserk when they heard the cracks of the bullets going off and saw us running out of the shelter and round to the banking like scared rabbits.

We were all playing around the air raid shelter below Walker's Pillar one evening when I went inside to hide. In the semi darkness, I noticed something shining in the corner, half hidden with some rags. Curious,

I went over and brushed away the rags and was surprised to find a saxophone. I took it outside and shouted to my pals.

We all marched around the banking trying to blow it but couldn't because it was too big and heavy. We had it for about twenty minutes, and then a strange man came along and asked us for it because he claimed it had been stolen from Minnie Boyle's house. We gave it to him and he thanked us, and gave us a penny each as a reward. We were delighted and ran to Minnie Boyle's shop to buy sweets. Little did we know then that the stranger was actually the thief who had taken the instrument from Minnie's but at least she got a few coppers back from us in recompense.

Home Guards

Many of the young local men were joining the army and the Home Guards. My half-brother Mickey, then about seventeen, and other young lads of his age that he palled with, joined the medical section of the local voluntary defence core. He and Dixie Dean and Patsy O'Brien, both from lower Nailor's Row, and my cousin Willie Lynch from Fox's Corner, were issued with long black coats and tin helmets. They wore a white armband with a Red Cross on it and a shoulder bag which contained bandages and cotton wool.

We stood and watched from the top of the banking when they were practising giving first aid to 'injured' civilians during a civil defence exercise. It all looked so real to us and we didn't find it a bit amusing at the time, except for the occasion when they were carrying a pretend injured man up the steep banking on the stretcher. The man at the back slipped and the three of them, along with the stretcher, went tumbling back down to the bottom of the banking. Fortunately, none of them was injured. As part of the exercises, stuffed dummies were placed on some of the house roofs. It reminded me of the film *Beau Geste* when the French Foreign Legion soldiers propped dead Legionaries on the ramparts of their fort to bluff the enemy attackers.

It made me aware of the reality of the war, especially at night whenever the sirens wailed as the German planes droned overhead on their way to bomb Belfast or us. Then we hurried, frightened, to the safety of the air raid shelters and many hid under their stairs and beds until the long wail of the all-clear siren was heard. Only then could we all go back to sleep safely in our beds.

Johnny McGill lived in upper Nailor's Row and regularly walked my father's greyhounds. Johnny was a tall slim man and always had a pleasant smile and a twinkle in his eyes. He was of a quiet nature and wore a brown brimmed hat, but only had one arm; he lost the other in the war when he was in the trenches in Borneo. The Japanese soldiers overran them and he pretended to be dead but had a bayonet stuck through his arm, which later had to be amputated. I loved to go out a walk with Johnny and the greyhounds up through Bligh's Lane and into the fields where we would slip off their leashes and let them run free.

One day, as I was toasting a piece of bread at the fire, I said to my mother, "Johnny McGill has only one arm, you know." I hadn't noticed Johnny sitting in the corner beside the dresser and when I turned around to look at my mother, he was smiling at me. I was very embarrassed, even at my young age, and ran out into the front street.

Those were the war years when many young men from the area joined the British army just to earn a few bob, get clothed and fed, and to escape from the poverty trap. Many of them never came home again, and we often saw the post office messenger delivering a telegram containing the sad news of another lost son to an anxious mother.

Two brothers, 'Spider' and 'Gander' Scanlon, from a family in Walker's Square, came home and ended their days begging for money to buy alcohol. One of them did menial work cleaning out rubbish and collecting returnable bottles for a livelihood. The other I found dead in the gutter at the top of Long Tower Street many years later, the street where he had played when he was a boy. Spider was his nickname, a name he got in his younger days when he did a bit of boxing. He was not related to the famous father and son boxers, Spider Kelly, who lived in Fahan Street.

View from the Royal Bastion, overlooking lower Nailor's Row in the 1940s. (Courtesy David Bigger collection.)

Smuggling and Sirens

All household commodities were scarce during the war years and every family had an official government ration book. A ration coupon was handed to the shopkeeper, along with some money, to purchase items such as tea, sugar, tobacco, snuff and clothing when they were available.

The Irish Republic was neutral during the war and Derry people travelled to and fro across the border to smuggle the necessities by bus, bicycle and train. The majority walked the few miles to County Donegal, usually in the late evening when darkness was falling. The British customs men set up checkpoints to catch people taking their meagre purchases home and often confiscated any goods they discovered. It was a form of highway robbery because there were many stories about confiscated goods being taken home by some of the customs men for their own use.

Women and children went on the train to get some goods for themselves and their neighbours. When they were returning, they sometimes hung their shopping bags full of contraband on the outside door handles of the train, on the side away from the station platform, so the customs men wouldn't find them when they came aboard to search. Sometimes a suspicious official looked out of the window to see the outside of the train lined with full shopping bags, and sometimes he pretended not to see them and waved to the train driver to continue on his journey to sighs of relief from the nervous passengers.

During those war years, fruit was scarce in the shops and in October, lorries came from Armagh loaded with apples from the orchards. Whenever one came into our street, everybody queued to buy a bucketful for a shilling. It was a great treat to eat a couple of juicy apples or to get a piece of apple pie that my mother baked in the fire oven. Sometimes she would give us a piece of dough that was left over and we would make a couple of small apple tarts to cook along with the cakes or pies.

After the war had ended, a variety of fruits started to arrive in the shops. On one occasion, Paddy, who drove a fruit lorry for Bannigan's fruit and vegetable store on Foyle Street, brought home a bunch of bananas. He gave me one and I began to eat it without removing the skin; it tasted horrible! After he stopped laughing and told me that it had to be peeled, I enjoyed the taste of it. The only place I had seen bananas before was in the school geography books about Africa.

Cigarettes, as well as many other commodities, were scarce during the war and people smuggled them across the border from County Donegal. One day, Willie heard that a shop at the bottom of Howard's Street was selling Turkish 'Pasha' cigarettes so he sent me to get him some. When I eventually got back home with the cigarettes, Willie eagerly lit one up. He immediately started to choke because they were such a rotten taste and he threw them into the bin. When Willie wasn't looking, Freddie and I took the cigarettes out of the bin and went around to the banking where about six of us lit some of them up and nearly choked ourselves to death. That was our only attempt at smoking until the war was well over.

During and after the war years, Derry's Lough Foyle was used as a NATO naval base, and when all the ships were in the port after taking part in sea manoeuvres, hundreds of sailors of every nationality would be out on the town looking for fun and romance. At the back of Friel's Terrace, on the top of the banking, there was a big tin hut called the 'Oaks'. It was used as a dance hall and housey (bingo) hall. Later on in the evenings, when it got dark, some of the sailors and local girls would kiss and cuddle behind our back yard walls beside the Oaks. For a laugh, we would often throw water over the wall at the courting couples and listen to them shouting threats and swearing at us. We would be bent over trying to hold in our giggling as we ran out through the house to the front street in case our parents would find out what we were up to and not let us go out again that night.

A blackout was strictly enforced at dusk during the war; the street lamps were never lit and every householder had to cover the insides of their windows with black blinds at night in case any German aircraft saw the light and bombed the town. Motor vehicles had to have hoods put on their lights to deflect the beams downwards and all torch lamps had to be directed to the ground.

Wardens patrolled the streets and if they saw a chink of light coming from a window, one of them hammered on the door of the house and warned the occupant to cover up properly or be prosecuted. On moonlit nights, everywhere was bathed in a soft light, and I could look down from our landing window at all the silver rooftops in the Bogside below.

Summer nights brought their own light, with the setting sun still giving out its golden glow into the wee small hours of the morning. Of course, we didn't see it very often when we were young because we were fast asleep before ten o'clock.

As things were scarce then, and ballpoint pens were not yet invented, Mickey made ink for our pens with water and red or black dyes that he stored in glass bottles. Every night, when we were all in bed, my mother came into our room in the dark and sprinkled us with holy water to keep us safe from all harm and evil. One morning, she came in to wake us for school and when she saw us, she blessed herself and said, "My God, what has happened to you all, have you all got the measles?" We didn't know what she was talking about until we got up and looked at each other. We couldn't understand it; we were all covered in red spots but none of us felt sick. Then she realised what had happened; she had sprinkled us with some of Mickey's red ink instead of the holy water, and we all had a good laugh for a long time afterwards whenever we talked about it.

"I hope the next bus to Derry comes soon." Baby twins in Springtown Camp in the 1940s. (Courtesy Mrs Stanley.)

Two beautiful ladies in Springtown enjoying the sunshine in the 1950s.
(Courtesy Mrs Stanley.)

Mrs Jennings with her two children at the door of their home in Springtown Camp in the 1950s. (Courtesy Mrs Stanley.)

Yanks in Springtown

An American military lorry came into the street one day and all the local children were placed on board under the canvas canopy. We were taken to the American camp at Springtown, near the Buncrana Road. I didn't know at the time where we were. Inside the camp, we sat at long tables with hundreds of other children and were given pastry and candy and ice cream. It was a very special treat for us in those days of strict rationing. Then we were all taken into another part of the camp where we watched cartoons of Mickey Mouse and Donald Duck. Afterwards, the lorry took us all home again, each of us clutching a small bag of sweets. I later learned that the Americans were celebrating Independence Day and that was why we were given the special treat.

When the war ended, the Americans abandoned the camp, leaving about eighty empty Nissen huts behind. A lot of people from our area, and especially Fahan Street, went to live in the huts. It was like moving into a mansion, especially for a family who had been living in terrible conditions in one room of a house with no electricity that was home to maybe six families who all had to share the one outside toilet.

Springtown was therefore seen as a good place to live until eventually, the huts began to deteriorate and conditions worsened again for the residents. Derry Corporation and the Rural County Council disowned the place and the people had to fend for themselves for years. They had to fight and agitate for better housing and social acceptance but that is a story better left for the ex-Springtown people to tell themselves.

Yankee Boats and an Irish Colleen

Whenever the American navy ships were taking part in manoeuvres and the North Atlantic Defence Fleet docked at the quay, we used to go to the jetties in the late evenings and stand at the foot of the gangplanks. There were a few other boys from the Bridge Street and Sugarhouse Lane areas there too that I still remember called 'Okay' Barratt, Billy 'Gurky' Gallagher, Dickie Valley and the two Doherty brothers, nicknamed 'Blabber' and 'Fly'. We were all hoping to do some paid errands for the sailors whom we referred to as the 'Yanks'.

Whenever the Yanks came to the bottom of the gangplank, we surrounded them, each of us hoping to be the lucky person to be sent into the town to purchase small food items, usually a dozen doughnuts and a pint of milk, or the odd bottle of Irish whiskey. The pint of milk and dozen doughnuts that we called gravy rings, cost about a half crown and the sailor would give us a five-dollar bill, which was worth twenty-five shillings, and tell us to keep the change whenever we returned with his order. It was an easy way for us to earn some pocket money and at the end of the evening, my friends and I shared our tips out evenly between us. Occasionally, one of the boys, when asked to bring a bottle of whiskey, would fill an empty one with black tea and swindle the unsuspecting sailor out of his dollars.

The two Doherty brothers, Fly and Blabber, who were with the Bridge Street boys, used to sing Irish ballads for the sailors in Bill Dalton's Bar in Rossville Street, and were recorded singing by Bill on his reel-to-reel tape recorder.

One evening when we were at the quay, a sailor asked Fly and Blabber to get him an Irish colleen. He gave them money to bring the colleen in a taxi to him when he came off duty. There happened to be a local female character about the town then called Maggie MacKay who was over fifty, but to us she seemed to be nearly a hundred. She wore a long dress and had a shawl around her head and shoulders, a style that was then still common in the western parts of Donegal. Fly and Blabber brought Maggie to the dock in the taxi and when the sailor looked inside, he screwed up his face when he beheld his wrinkled Irish colleen laid out on the back seat. She was smiling with gaps in her teeth and fluttering her eyelids at him from under her shawl. "Holy Moley," he exclaimed, "if that's what you call an Irish colleen, then my old grand-mother must be a beauty queen."

Some Nelson Street residents in the 1940s. (Courtesy Rev B Canning.)

Bamboozalem Magic

Bamboozalem was an illusionist whose magic act was the talk of the town and everybody was amazed at his show. He could make things disappear and ropes stand unaided. He could take coins out of people's ears and make birds fly out of his hands. He could vanish from the stage in a cloud of smoke and he astounded people so much that many said he must have been in league with some spiritual being.

His marquee was in Watt's field behind the Lecky Road, later renamed Meenan's Park after the councillor who procured it for the city to make it into a park. My mother and father took us to see Bamboozalem. His tent had a low ceiling and was crowded. I was so excited watching the birds fly from his hands and seeing the coloured smoke rising from the stage and dulling the bright lights above his head. His act was amazing and certainly bamboozled me!

Ghandi

A familiar sight in the city was James 'Ghandi' Hughes from Strabane who lost both of his legs when a train struck him as he worked on the railroads in Canada. He wore a thick canvas sack over the lower part of his body and tied around his waist. The bottom of the sack was attached to a flat circular board with small wheels on which he propelled himself along using a wooden block in each hand. I learned that he lived in a tin hut and that he travelled around Strabane on a small cart that was pulled by a large horned goat. He was a very bad tempered man and we were warned to keep well away from him whenever he came into our street.

The Phantom and Other Characters

There was a well-dressed young man who came into the street in the evenings now and then riding a big black bicycle with its wheels and spokes shining like silver and its frame well polished. He was known

They don't make tricycles like that anymore. Cycling from Abbey Street down Thomas Street in 1945. (Courtesy Eddie Moore.)

only as the Phantom. He performed figures of eight on his bicycle by riding towards the wall or pavement, and just at the last second, he swerved around to do the same manoeuvre on the opposite side of the road again. The Phantom continued doing the figures of eight until he got to the other end of the street and then disappeared just as quickly as he had arrived. He never spoke to anyone, and the only sound that was heard was the humming of the tyres on the road and the clicking of the chain and cogwheels from his bicycle. He gave the same display in other parts of the town as well.

Another man was called 'Cut the Corners' because of his slyness. He collected debt money for a local shop and whenever he came into a street, he always kept very close to the corner so he could quickly spot any woman standing at her door before she had a chance to spot him and dart inside to avoid paying her dues. Anyone seeing him would shout out, "Here comes Cut the Corners," to warn the debt dodgers he was coming.

There was a woman who passed down the street every day and she was known as 'Figaroo' because she wore a very tight-fitting coat that looked too small for her. Another woman who passed along the street once in a while got the nickname 'Cacky Heels' because her heels were a dirty brown colour above her shoes.

Other names that people were tagged with were: Yellow Ned, who had a yellow-brown coloured neck; Dan the Rand; Beezebull's Eye; Johnny Cuttems, who worked for Hawker Lynch; Johnny the German; Barney Bugles; Bella Scads. Other nicknames included Cocoa Hole, Slabbery Mickey, Flannel Feet, Cow Walloper, Half-moon Dan, Creeping Jesus, Dixie Dean, Scouse, Douse, Ming, Magwah, and Long Trams. There was also: Biddy with the Wooden Diddy, Hairy Jaws, Willie Turf and Tommy Tit.

A bad mannered person was a 'gulpin', a sturdy looking girl would give you a 'good hoult', and an awkward clumsy one was a 'big hallion'. A person who wore a pair of trousers that were too big for him (which were probably hand-me-downs from a bigger brother or his father) was called 'long trams'. At times a person would be seen with a hole in the backside of his trousers and his shirt tail sticking out through the hole, then someone would give the protruding tail a tug to the man's or boy's embarrassment. That was the trend at the time and if any of those people were in any kind of difficulty, their neighbours were at their doors to help them because they were the ones who put a sparkle into the daily lives of the people in the locality.

The Slipper Gang

There were three older boys in the area who were known as the 'Slipper Gang'. They stole small things from the shops, mostly sweets and bars of chocolate. One day, one of them pointed up the Walls to show us where they had hidden some of their loot. We could see a box of chocolates sticking out of the mouth of a cannon, just in the front of Walker's Pillar. When he left, we tried to climb up to get them as sweets were scarce then because of the war. We were craving to get them but we couldn't reach and none of us was brave enough to edge out along the cannon to get them.

We found out later that the Slipper Gang had stolen some bullets from a parked police car and dumped them on the banking – the same bullets that nearly shot our heads off in the air raid shelter when we threw them onto the fire!

Winker

Living in a street below the banking was an ex-sailor known as Winker, and he kept women lodgers who went out with sailors. It was a common sight to see the sailors entering and leaving the house with the women. A lot of the girls dated sailors off the ships that docked on the quay in those days and many got married to them and settled down in Derry, or went to America to live.

One morning, news spread that Winker had been found dead in the house. As was the custom here, Winker was laid out in his coffin to be waked in his house and the neighbours visited to pay their respects as usual.

We happened to be playing on the banking at the time and we heard a commotion coming from Winker's street. Cathal shouted to us, "Come on quick till we see what's happening," so we all ran down into the street from where we heard the din. There were a few British sailors and some women and a priest arguing outside Winker's front door, and there, sitting on a chair with his cap on and a pipe in his mouth, was the cause of all the commotion – Winker himself! The sailors had taken the corpse out of the coffin and put it outside the house. It had been an act of desecration and everybody was annoyed about the incident for a long while after.

Ba' in the Spoot

'Ba' in the Spoot' was a nickname given to a Scotsman who worked as a handyman for the owner of the houses in Friel's Terrace. During the rainy weather, the gutters on the roofs always flowed over and he and his assistant had to fix them. One day, he climbed up the ladder to a gutter to investigate why it was overflowing and discovered that the downspout was blocked, so he shouted to his partner, "It's a ba' in the spoot," meaning 'it's a ball in the spout' that was causing the blockage and that's how he got his nickname.

Hawker Lynch and Johnny Cuttems

Hawker Lynch was a very intelligent and witty man who often went down our street. He was a tall thin man who wore a cap and he had thick lenses in his spectacles. He was a regular at the Derry matches in the Brandywell where he entertained the other spectators with his witty remarks. A self-employed poster writer and advertiser, he used the services of Johnny 'Cuttems' McLaughlin to walk around the town wearing sandwich boards with advertisements stuck on them. Hawker didn't have had a well-paid job because he wasn't properly educated and came from the wrong side of the town.

One day Hawker was standing on the Guildhall steps, waiting for

Johnny Cuttems, when a couple of local lads thought they would pull his leg. One of them said to Hawker, "Hi, Hawker, did you see a cartload of monkeys going past?" Hawker replied sharply, " Sure I did, and have you fallen off it?"

A few other humorous stories demonstrate Hawker's sharp wit.

Johnny was to advertise for Hawker at the Brandywell show grounds one day, but before he donned the sandwich boards, he asked Hawker how he was to be paid; per day, per week or per month? Hawker swiftly replied, without even blinking an eye, "Per-haps."

At a soccer match between Derry and Linfield in the Brandywell one Saturday, Hawker was getting fed up listening to some of the Linfield supporters from Belfast singing *The Sash,* and in a lull he shouted to the singers, "Youse are singing away about Derry, Aughrim, Enniskillen and the Boyne but how come the song doesn't even mention your wee Belfast?" They were silent for a few minutes after that as they mumbled to one another and then they began to sing *No Surrender.*

Funnies and Cowboys

Skinny Malinky Doodle Ump, big banana feet,
Went to the pictures to get himself a seat.
When he got a seat, he fell fast asleep.
Skinny Malinky Doodle Ump, big banana feet.

In Gallagher's Close, a little square off Fox's Corner, was the Matt Talbot Hall or shed that was so named after a saintly alcoholic who began a crusade to educate young people about the dangers and heartaches caused by the excessive drinking of alcohol. On late Sunday evenings, it cost three pence to see films there starring The Dead End Kids, Laurel and Hardy, the Three Stooges or Charlie Chaplin. The shed was always packed and sometimes, whenever the film was on, some smart Alec would put their hand up in front of the beam from the film projector which blocked the image showing on the screen. This would cause an uproar and everyone would shout at him to get his hand down. The film broke down quite often and the noisy crowd

Like many other streets in Derry, there was great neighbourliness amongst these residents of Cable Street, pictured here receiving an award for the cleanest street in the city in 1966. (Courtesy *Derry News*.)

stamped and jeered until the fault was rectified. I remember Barney and Paddy Harkin, who lived in Fox's Corner, Skinny and Bernie O'Neill, Tommy Long and the McDonald brothers, Tony and Columba from the Wells, along with many of the other men who lived in the vicinity, keeping order during the performances when people and machinery started acting up.

Cinemas were called picture houses and the movies called pictures by most of the Derry cinemagoers. So a person would say they were going to the City picture house to see the big picture and the wee picture, which meant they were going to see the main film and the supporting short film. The pictures were mostly in black and white, and talkies were not very long invented, so lots of movies were still silent and captions were inserted in each scene for the spectators to read what the actors were saying. In those days also, a high number of people couldn't read and it was so funny listening to the dozens of literate people reading aloud in the picture house so the non-readers could follow the story.

Another very funny occasion was when the 'baddie' was hiding behind the door in the room waiting to pounce on the hero and everyone got excited and screamed up at the screen, "Look out, he's behind the door." Or whenever the baddie got the better of the hero, curses and abuse were hurled up at the villain along with the odd few apple stumps.

When we were old enough, about seven or eight, Freddie and Danny and I were allowed to go with our pals to the pictures in St Columb's Hall. We didn't have any sweets or fruit with us and we queued up with the hundreds of other boys to watch our heroes, Gene Autry, Roy Rodgers, Gabby Hayes, Smiley Burnett and Fuzzy Knights. Strangely, there never seemed to be any girls in the queue or in the hall to see the movies. The cowboys rode their horses called Champion, Trigger, Ring Eye or Mule; they caught the baddies, saved the girls, and helped the sheriff. They were always smiling and singing and never kissed the girls. They were everyone's friends and heroes.

Other cowboys were the Lone Ranger and Tonto; Charles Starret, alias the Durango Kid, and Jellybeans; Hopalong Cassidy and Topper, his horse. Tom Mix and Lash Laroo were also exciting, but none of them ever matched Gene Autry and Roy Rodgers whose hats never fell off, even when they jumped from their horses or when they were fighting.

Whenever we got home and had our tea after the matinee, the banking was our range and as cowboys and Indians, we would ride and shoot at each other and play dead until sunset. Then, contentedly wounded and tired, we would put our guns and battle-axes away until the next week. It was time to get washed and scrubbed clean in the big tin bath in front of the glowing fire and have our clean clothes and polished brogues laid out for Mass the next morning.

Songs and Music

One day when I was about five years old, Mickey brought home a harmonica. We called it a French fiddle or a mouth organ in those days. It was striking to look at with its gleaming silver sides and two rows of tiny square holes for blowing into. Whenever Mickey played it, it made the sweetest musical harmony I had ever heard, apart from the accordion, and I wanted so much to master it too. After a few days, Mickey got fed up with it and let me have it. It was to be my most precious possession and I practised every day, with my mother's encouragement, until I was able to play every tune that was in my young head. By the time I was seven, I could play all the Orange music I had heard on Derry's Walls and all the Irish tunes, marches and popular songs of that era. My repertoire included songs by the two greatest Irish tenors, John McCormack and Joseph Locke; American singer Paul Robeson's songs, *Old Man River* and *That Lucky Old Sun*; and tunes by American quartet The Ink Spots who sang *Whispering Grass*.

Two other popular American songs of the period were *Nickelodeon*, which was a jukebox that played records in American cafés, and *Mares eat oats and does eat oats and little lambs eat ivy, a kid'll eat ivy too, wouldn't you?* Those were what I took to be the lyrics of the first catchy American song to hit Derry, made popular by the Andrew Sisters.

One of my older brothers sometimes got the loan of a gramophone which had to be wound up by turning a handle before each record (or disc) was played. The records were about twelve inches in diameter and made of a brittle Bakelite material. They had only one song or tune on each side and had to be played at 78 revolutions per minute (rpm). The gramophone needles had to be renewed after every two songs and were bought in boxes of a hundred. My brother always got the loan of the same six or seven records of Joseph Locke and Al Jolsen, and a couple with marching bands music. There was one song I remember I listened to many times, about two little orphans sitting by an old church door, and it was very sad.

We listened to the gramophone for hours each night and it was funny to hear the singer's voice getting lower and lower whenever the spring gradually lost its tension. Then one of us would rush to wind it up again as the record kept on playing and we would hear the voice and the music climbing to reach full pitch again. It was even funnier when my father was listening to his favourite marching band and my mother would say in jest, whenever the pitch lowered, "They must be playing the dead march."

Bags of Coke

After the tin paling that separated Howard's Place from the banking was knocked down, we were able to go straight through to Maggie Campbell's front room shop in Howard's Place to buy the 'Free State' sweets and bubble gum. It was also a short cut for Freddie and me whenever we were sent to the Gasworks yard in the Brandywell on Saturday mornings to get bags of coke for the fire. Coke was what was left over after coal had gone through the distillation process to create the gas that was stored in huge tanks called gasometers and then piped to the houses and other buildings in Derry for lighting and cooking.

The coke was stacked in huge mountains in the yard and sometimes the new heaps caught fire and the workers had to hose the flames with water. When the water poured onto the burning coke, it gave off a putrid smell and the rotten taste of the fumes would linger in my mouth for hours after. On windy days, bits of dust and coke were blown everywhere and it was very painful if a particle went into your eye and

Queuing for bags of coke outside the Gasworks gate in the Lecky Road with Barman Duffy at the entrance keeping people in order in the 1940s. (Courtesy David Bigger collection.)

you rubbed it. I often had to get my mother to bathe my eyes to remove the stinging dust.

The man who usually controlled the queue for the coke was Barman Duffy and no one dared to sneak ahead whenever he was at the gate. We queued up with hundreds of other boys and men of all ages, all with a sack draped over an arm in which to carry home the coke on their back if they were lucky enough to live near hand. I had a trolley made out of pram wheels and wood to help me get my load home and some people even used the babies' prams themselves (but they took the babies out first!).

Whenever I reached the front of the queue, I went over to the man beside the stack of coke and gave him my ticket. He shovelled the coke into a large scoop that sat on top of the scales and weighed a bushel and told me to hold the mouth of the sack under the scoop. He then tipped the coke into the sack in one swift movement and the sudden weight nearly pulled it out of my grasp. Then I dragged the sack over to lift it onto my trolley with Freddie's help.

When we were ready, we had to push the trolley across the Wells, up Howard's Street, and across the banking until we reached Friel's Terrace. Then we would carry the bag in through the house to the coal shed in the back yard. When our day's work was done, my mother gave us sixpence each to go to the matinee in St Columb's Hall to see our cowboy heroes. We were happy with our reward and would have done it for nothing anyway.

Electioneering

One-two-three aleera, I spy De Valera,
Sitting on his bumbaleera, eating chocolate biscuits.

During election time, there were hundreds of people out listening to the candidates making their speeches. The Nationalists were Paddy Fox, Doctor Cavanagh, James Doherty and Eddie McAteer whose brother Hugh had escaped from Crumlin Road Jail in Belfast along with other Republican prisoners. I remember our teacher introducing him to us in

John Hume, the then newly elected Westminster MP, addresses a crowd of his supporters on the Lecky Road in 1970; in the background is lower Nailor's Row and Friel's Terrace at the top of the snow-covered banking. (Courtesy Rev B Canning.)

President of Ireland Eamon De Valera heading a parade at the opening of a Gaelic cultural festival in Derry in 1951. Walking behind his car are Councillors Paddy Maxwell, Eddie McAteer, James Hegarty, James Doherty, Paddy Fox and Pat Meenan.
(Courtesy Eddie Moore.)

school one day and was fascinated when he spoke about some of his experiences in jail.

One Nationalist candidate spoke from a platform erected in the Little Diamond with an Irish Tricolour fluttering above it. The spectators cheered loudly after his every sentence and the children used to chant, "Up the rebels, up the rebels, up the leg of your drawers." We never heard any of the opposing candidates speaking, some of whose names I can just barely remember, such as Ross, McFarland, Anderson and Glover.

Ned's Donkey Cart

There were two donkeys that grazed on the banking along with Johnny McDermott's white horse. Nobody ever annoyed them as they quietly munched away, and sometimes they came round into the street to look for tit bits or some bread. The women of the street always chased them back to their own territory in case they would clatter into their houses, which they occasionally did in search of food. The donkeys belonged to Ned McDevitt from Fox's Corner who led them off the banking every evening down to his house where he brought them in through the front door, through the hall to the back room and out into the yard for the night.

One time Ned built a new cart for his donkeys in his back yard. Everybody was wondering how he was going to get it out to the street because he had no exit from the backyard beside Adam's Close so this was the talk of the neighbours. When the job was finally completed and the paint was dry, a crane from the docks rolled up Rossville Street and turned into Fox's Corner. It stopped at Ned's front door and, with its jib stretching over the roof of the house, a hook was slowly lowered into the back yard. The new donkey cart was rigged up to the hook, hoisted high over Ned's roof, and then lowered gently into the front street to the appreciative applause of the onlookers.

A grotto to honour the Virgin Mary near the bottom of Bishop Street, one of the many that were built in Derry in the early 1950s. Back standing, from left: Jim O'Donnell and J Ward. Kneeling: John McKinney and John McCarron. Sitting front, from left: Willie Bradley, W Kearney, Unknown, Pascal Keys, B McAnaney, Joe Keys and Mickey Rooney.

A group in New Street off Bishop Street includes: John Doherty, Willie Gallagher and Kevin Barratt. Front right: Willie 'Spaldy' Doherty and Pat Meehan.

What Are Youse?

Oh, as I was walking down the street
I saw King William fighting.
So I jumped on his back
And I gave him a whack
And he ran away like lightning.

When I got older, at about eight or nine, I was able to drift away from the banking along with my pals to explore other parts of the town. One particular evening we discovered that exploration could be dangerous as well as exciting.

Five of us were walking down past the bottom of Bishop Street when were confronted by a small bunch of boys of our own age group. They stood in front of us to stop us and we prepared to push them aside. Then we heard a shout from behind and looked round. To our horror, a gang of about eight bigger boys was coming towards us and we just stood there, sandwiched between the two groups, hopelessly trapped.

Nothing like that would ever happen to us on the banking where we could outrun any outsider on the rough and hilly terrain, and then stone them out of our domain. But we weren't on the banking now, we were in strange unknown territory where we were going to get battered, and Cathal wasn't even with us to challenge the leader of the aggressors as he always did whenever we were in a jam. Unfortunately for us, he had to whitewash the back yard for his mother and couldn't come with us that day.

The gang made us stand with our backs against the wall and started shouting at us. Then one of them ordered the others to be quiet and he asked us, "Are youse Protestants or Catholics?" Three of us said that we were Catholics, and the other two said nothing, in case we should have said we were Protestants. To test us, we were told to say the Our Father, and we recited it one at a time. After the first two of us had nervously stumbled through the prayer, a couple of the bigger boys said to the rest of them, "Let them go, they're Catholics." It was a very relieved and chastened gang of five that went on its way with some valuable experience gained the hard way.

Moving News

When I reached the age of twelve, my days of playing on the banking and the back of the Walls came to an end. We came in from school one day and my mother broke the news to us that we had been allocated a four-bedroom house in the newly built Creggan Estate.

There were fifteen of us living in the house at that time and it was a great future that awaited us in our brand new house in Creggan with an electric light in every room and a kitchen with a sink and hot and cold running water. There was an inside toilet and a separate bathroom too, with a bath and a wash hand basin, each with hot and cold taps. We were going to have a garden for growing vegetables at the back of the house and a front garden for grass and flowers. There would be plenty of exploring and investigating on the first few days in our new house.

What a change it was going to be from our little house with two bedrooms and one sitting room-cum-bedroom. How different it would be from our living room with the hard wooden sofa and the old pinewood dresser with its white plates and bowls and hanging cups that reflected the firelight from the glowing coke in the grate. Maybe we would miss our cosy wee home where we bathed in the big tin bath in front of the fire, where Julia and my mother did all the baking and cooking, and where we ate at the scrubbed white wooden table with the four wooden chairs around it.

No more telling stories when the gaslight cosily hissed in the dark evenings as it spread its gentle soft blanket of light over the room that held so many memories for my family and me. No more sitting on the shining fire fender, or running in my bare feet out to the toilet in the yard, or carrying in buckets of water for washing and cooking. And no more rushing up the dark stairs at bedtime hoping that my Guardian Angel was protecting me from the Bogey Man as I knelt to say my prayers before diving into bed and the safety of my blankets.

The Flit

It was with very mixed emotions that my parents said goodbye to their neighbours. Although they were happy to have a new life in Creggan, they regretted leaving many childhood friends whom they had good times and endured many hardships with over the years, when everyone helped each other, and shared what they could afford.

We, the younger ones, also had our goodbyes to make to our friends and neighbours; the friends we had spent so many happy days with, playing on the banking, and climbing up Derry's Walls, and throwing stones up at our silent neighbour who still had his back to us on his lofty plinth.

The day we moved out of Friel's Terrace to our new house in Creggan, it was a soft warm June evening with the sun still high in the south-western sky. Freddie and I were on the back of the lorry with Paddy driving it. Neighbours were waving their goodbyes and a little group of our pals of all ages gathered at the top of the banking. They just watched in silence as we moved off towards Fahan Street on the short journey to our new modern life, and the beginning of my adolescence, in the new Creggan Estate.

As we drove away, I looked up to Nailor's Row and a solitary figure was standing there in the middle of the street, watching me in motionless silence. I waved to him and, smiling shyly, Cathal nodded his head, knowing that we were still friends and there would still be many days ahead when we would go exploring in the fields and countryside together; up Bligh's Lane and into the meadows to look for birds' nests and frogs spawn and sticklebacks; away from beneath the shadow of the Walls, and Governor Walker on his pillar, and the black cannons ever pointing into our lives on the top of the banking. Cathal, our protector and my best friend, who later would be gone forever from us in his innocent youth.

"I wish we had some bullets for this gun." Boys on a cannon in the Double Bastion on Derry's Walls, overlooking Nailor's Row and Friel's Terrace. (Courtesy E Melaugh http://cain.ulst.ac.uk/melaugh/)

A Twilight Memory
by Phil Cunningham

Broken slates and shattered stones,
All scattered now, where once stood homes.
All gone, 'neath shadow of the Walls,
Now gone, but what the mind recalls.
The banking, where met friend or foe,
To play, to fight, or to greet and know.
All gone, those happy carefree days
Of innocence, and gentle ways.
When just a little prayer or touch,
Could ease the heart and mean so much.
All gone those days, and gone forever.
But from my heart I shall lose them never.